PSYCHOLOGY

FOR **AS** LEVEL

WORKBOOK

CLARE CHARLES
North Leamington School, Leamington Spa

Psychology Press
Taylor & Francis Group

HOVE AND NEW YORK

Published in 2002 by Psychology Press Ltd
27 Church Road, Hove, East Sussex, BN3 2FA

http://www.psypress.co.uk
http://www.a-levelpsychology.co.uk

Simultaneously published in the USA and Canada
by Taylor & Francis Inc
270 Madison Avenue, New York, NY 10016

Psychology Press is part of the Taylor & Francis Group

Reprinted 2003, 2004

British Library Cataloguing in Publication Data
A catalogue record for this book is available from the British Library

ISBN 1-84169-332-4

Typeset in the UK by Facing Pages, Southwick, West Sussex
Printed and bound in the UK by Ashford Colour Press

Contents

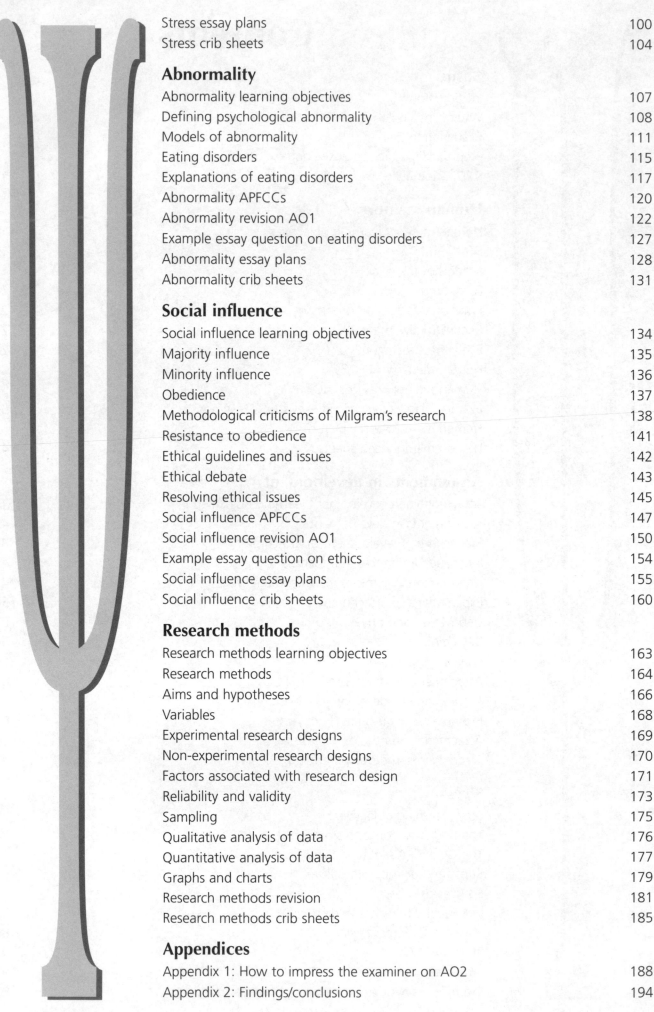

Introduction

Hello

I hope you have begun to think about how to get that C grade or above at AS level psychology. This workbook is here to help you do it. That's no guarantee you'll get the grade you want, of course, because you must use the workbook thoroughly to get a good pass. Empty pages mean empty spaces—great big gaps in your knowledge that not even the revision guide will necessarily fill in. This workbook does require some commitment from you—there are notes to be made and model answers to prepare. But then that is the only way to get the AS grade you deserve!

After a brief discussion of the different areas and approaches to studying psychology, the first section of the workbook is focused on examination skills. The AO1, AO2, and AO3 exam skills are considered in terms of the type of exam question they may be assessed by. The APFCC (Aims, Procedures, Findings, Conclusions, Criticisms) template provides guidance on how to approach the exam questions that ask for research studies to be described. There is also a step-by-step guide to answering exam questions.

Each of the following sections of the workbook is organised in the same way:

- **Learning objectives** introduce each of the topics. Cross reference with the Specification so that you can see how the learning objectives meet the requirements of the Specification. Please fill in the self-assessment box on completion of a topic as it is often useful for your own revision and the class programme to have a record of the parts of the Specification that may need close attention during revision.

- **Structured worksheets** that map on to each of the learning objectives. These can be used by you for independent study or be used as a stimulus to guide discussion and note taking in class if selected by your teacher. The worksheets include page references to Eysenck's *Psychology for AS Level, Third Edition* textbook and Brody and Dwyer's *Revise Psychology for AS Level* revision guide. The worksheets are structured because cues are given that direct note taking and help you to select only the most relevant content. You should be able to cross-reference these cues with the information in most AS textbooks, but they do relate specifically to the Eysenck textbook. Your note taking must be very concise to fit into the worksheets. This is an important skill to acquire because in the exam you will need to be equally succinct. At the end of each worksheet is a section that relates the content to how this might be assessed in the exam through examples of possible exam questions.

- **The APFCCs** (Aims, Procedures, Findings, Conclusions, Criticisms). There are 16 key studies that can be examined as advised by AQA (2005/2006 Specification A). The APFCCs suggest a suitable study and enable you to make your own notes. These should be used in conjunction with the APFCC template in this first section of the workbook, which suggests how to note relevant content. It is also possible to cross-reference with Eysenck's textbook or Brody and Dwyer's revision guide for the full APFCCs. Also complete the findings/conclusions (Appendix 2) for the key research areas in order to be prepared for 6-mark questions on either aspect.

- **Revision AO1 summaries** should be used as a checklist where you tick off the questions you have prepared a model answer for and feel confident you could answer well. The revision summaries include a list of the definition questions that can be cross-referenced with the glossary in the back of the Brody and Dwyer revision guide. They also include a list of research studies (in APFCC format), explanations/theories, comparison, and criticisms questions, which try to comprehensively cover the range of possible AO1 exam questions. Guidance on the answers is suggested with reference to the worksheets.

- **Example 18-mark essay questions**. A model answer is included for each of the critical issues. Note the use of structure: the three-paragraph model, with a conclusion and bullet points, which act as cues to facilitate memory. Hopefully you will then use the three-paragraph model with bullet points as a framework for preparing model answers to the other AO2 questions identified on the worksheets.

- **Essay plans**. The plans hopefully cover the full range of possible essay questions. They are abbreviated answers that you need to expand in order to have a complete set of model answers. There is no right or wrong answer so the plans only provide advice on suitable content and structure; it is up to you how you choose to use them.

- **Crib sheets**. These sheets are a condensed version of each topic. Complete these and you will have detailed, comprehensive information, and fewer notes to revise from! They review and enable you to consolidate in memory the content that has been covered previously in the workbook. Use these in conjunction with the revision AO1 summaries, APFCCs, example essays, and essay plans to be fully prepared for any exam question.

Included in the Appendices is a worksheet called 'How to impress the examiner on AO2', which provides further ideas on how to do well on the essay questions, and a 'Findings/conclusions' summary for you to complete.

Good luck with your studies. I hope you do get the grade you deserve—and make sure you deserve a good one!

Clare Charles

Wherever possible we have provided enough space for you to fill in your answers. However, if you find that there is not enough room to do this, continue on a blank sheet of paper, or use the blank 'Notes' section at the end of the book.

What is Psychology?

Definition of psychology

There are five key areas within psychology: cognitive psychology, developmental psychology, physiological psychology, individual differences, and social psychology, and the topics you will study are drawn from these areas. Other areas that exist within the field of psychology include clinical, occupational, comparative, educational, criminal, and neuropsychology. In addition to these main areas, there are various approaches or perspectives to studying psychology: biological, behavioural, cognitive, and psychodynamic, which you will become familiar with during the course of your studies. Each approach takes a different view to explain psychological phenomena. Take a look at the worksheet that follows (see page 5) to find out more about these areas and approaches, which are fundamental to an understanding of psychology.

As you can see, psychology is diverse and challenging and so (nearly) always exciting!!!

Psychologists tend to specialise in a particular area of psychological research, such as children's acquisition of language, the nature and causes of aggression, or the development of moral reasoning. Some psychologists take a particular perspective, but most take an eclectic approach, which means that they draw from a broad range of theories and perspectives rather than being restricted to the approach of only one particular school of thought. This is because *no one theory in science is final*, hence the need to take a multi-perspective approach to studying psychology. This is considered by many to be the only way to deal successfully with the issues that psychologists address. The use of psychology in practical settings is called applied psychology, and the applications are based on research in one or more of the areas; for example, research into problem solving is based on cognitive psychology, and research into prejudice and discrimination is based on social psychology.

Here's a reminder of the five key areas that you are going to study at AS level:

Cognitive   Developmental   Physiological   Individual differences   Social

Look at the following applications and see if you can decide which area the application is most likely to be derived from. Discuss this with the people sitting next to you and complete the worksheet with the correct areas. In some cases the application could be based on more than one approach, as a multi-perspective approach may need to be taken, and so you may conclude that it is based on research from more than one of the five areas (detailed on page 5). In these cases write all relevant areas in the boxes below.

Applications

Ψ How to improve memory.

Ψ The causes of schizophrenia.

Ψ What is the basis of interpersonal attraction?

Ψ The relationship between stress and illness.

Ψ Why some people conform and others don't.

Ψ Brain wave activity during sleep.

Ψ The physiological basis of depression.

Ψ Gender differences in socialisation.

Ψ What is normal/is anybody normal?

Ψ Do dreams have meaning or are they just a by-product of brain activity?

Ψ The relationship between the infant and caregiver.

Ψ Artificial intelligence.

Ψ Causes of relationship breakdown.

Ψ Relaxation training.

Ψ Attention deficits.

Ψ Are psychopaths born that way or created by society?

Cognitive psychology

'Cognition' refers to our mental processes, such as attention, perception, thinking, language, and memory. Thus, cognitive psychology looks at how we process information to understand the thoughts that underpin emotions and behaviour. It can overlap with social psychology in the area of social cognition, or with developmental psychology in the area of cognitive development. This approach focuses on the brain as an information processor and computers can be used as an analogy of the brain to help develop mental models to explain and understand cognitive processes.

Developmental psychology

Developmental psychology studies the biological, cognitive, social, and emotional changes that occur throughout the life span. As development is a lifelong process, developmental psychologists start their study with conception and pre-natal development, then move from infancy through to adolescence, adulthood, and finally old age. Topics studied could involve early cognitive development, the attachments formed between infants and their caregivers, and the gender roles acquired in early childhood. The psychodynamic perspective links well to this area because it claims that unconscious childhood conflicts shape adult behaviour.

Physiological psychology

Physiological psychology aims to establish the biological basis of behaviour. Body structures and functions, in particular brain processing, are investigated to see how they relate to behaviour. For example, the body's response to stress is a good illustration of a behaviour that has a biological basis. Physiological psychologists study topics such as how the nerves function, how hormones affect behaviour, and how the different areas of the brain are specialised and related to different behaviours. The term 'biological' is used when referring to body structures and 'physiological' is used when referring to bodily processes.

Individual differences

As expected, individual differences looks at the wide variation in individuals. It deals with studying the ways in which individuals differ in their psychological characteristics, and this will affect their intelligence, aggressiveness, willingness to conform, masculinity and femininity, and just about every other behaviour you can think of. An important individual difference is the degree to which a person is mentally healthy, and this gives rise to the study of abnormal psychology. However, what is considered to be normal for one person may not be considered to be normal by another person. This means that there is huge controversy and ambiguity in defining abnormality. Within abnormal psychology mental disorders are investigated such as eating disorders, schizophrenia, depression, and anxiety disorders.

Social psychology

'Social' refers to any situation involving two or more members of the same species. Social psychology investigates social interactions, such as interpersonal relationships, group behaviour, leadership, social influence, and the influence of the media. A social psychologist studying interpersonal relationships might study what we find attractive in others or what causes relationships to deteriorate and end. One who is studying social influence might look at how others influence us, e.g., conformity and obedience to authority.

Examination Skills

This workbook provides a framework for useful learning and revision (the worksheets) and advice on how to develop the skills that will be assessed in the examination (the AO1 and AO2 revision summaries). AO1, AO2, and AO3 are the skills being assessed and the following descriptions reveal exactly what these requirements are and how to achieve high marks on all three assessment objectives.

AO1 tests knowledge and understanding

This means that there will be describe/outline questions that can be sub-divided into the following categories.

Ψ Definitions of key terms

Example exam questions:

Explain what is meant by the terms… and…	(3 + 3 marks)
Explain what is meant by the terms…, …, and…	(2 + 2 + 2 marks)

All key terms that could be asked for in the exam are identified in the AO1 revision summaries, and are also listed in blue in the 'Defining key terms and concepts' pages in Brody and Dwyer's revision guide.

Ψ Research studies (APFCC and findings/conclusions) questions

Example exam questions:

Describe the aims/procedures/findings/conclusions/one criticism of one study into…	(6 marks)
Describe the findings of one study into…	(6 marks)
Describe the conclusions of one study into…	(6 marks)
Give two criticisms of the research…	(3 + 3 marks)

Questions will ask for the aims, procedures, findings, conclusions, or criticisms of psychological studies. Any two of these could be asked for, i.e., aims and findings, procedures and one criticism, etc. Also, you may be asked for the findings or conclusions only so you need to have enough content on the findings or conclusions to get 6 marks. Or two criticisms may be asked for, where both criticisms would be allocated 3 marks. This may mean learning more than one study but this is not necessarily the case; for example, Milgram's obedience study would elicit sufficient content on its own. See the APFCC template and complete the APFCCs and findings/conclusions for each topic area to be fully prepared for any research question. Only the areas on the Specification preceded by 'research into' can come up as an APFCC question in the exam. There are 16 research areas, thus 16 APFCCs to learn, and this content can also be used in other AO1 questions and the essays. No study is specified on the Specification, which means you can choose which ones you learn. Hence, those suggested for you are only suggestions so if you know any others that are better then please use them instead.

Ψ Explanations/theories questions

Example exam questions:

Outline two effects of factors that explain or which influence …	(3 + 3 marks)
Outline two ways that explain or which influence…	(3 + 3 marks)
Outline two psychological processes that explain or which influence…	(3 + 3 marks)

Notice *two* is the 'magic number' for AO1. These questions are based on the Specification, which you should study closely because it contains all of the exam questions. For example, only the content on the Specification that is stated 'including' could be specified in an exam question, e.g., Bowlby's maternal deprivation hypothesis, the definitions of abnormality, the models of memory, and many more. Whereas, if the Specification content is preceded by 'e.g.' then it cannot be specified in an exam question. For example, this is the case with the explanations of forgetting and attachment. Thus, it is useful to know which content you could be asked specifically; whether it be to describe or criticise. See the AO1 revision summaries for a checklist of questions.

Ψ Comparison questions

Example exam questions:

Outline two differences between…	(3 + 3 marks)
Outline three similarities between…	(2 + 2 + 2 marks)

For similarities and differences, see the AO1 revision summaries.

Ψ Criticism questions

Example exam questions:

Give two criticisms of… research	(3 + 3 marks)
Give two criticisms of… APFCC	(3 + 3 marks)
Give two criticisms of… explanations/theories	(3 + 3 marks)

These criticisms can be positive and negative, i.e., strengths and weaknesses. All the structured worksheets contain evaluation and the methodological criticisms in the 'How to impress the examiner on AO2' appendix could also be used for AO1 criticism questions.

AO2 tests evaluation and analysis

Example exam questions:

Outline and consider the strengths and weaknesses…	(18 marks)
To what extent does psychological research (theories and/or studies) support/explain…	(18 marks)
Consider whether psychologists have been successful in explaining…	(18 marks)

Ψ 18-mark essay questions (6 AO1 marks, 12 AO2 marks)

The 18-mark essay question is always the final sub-part (c) of a question. The 6 AO1 marks require description; the 12 AO2 marks require evaluation and analysis. Evaluation requires you to assess the *strengths and weaknesses* of a concept, theory, explanation, or research evidence; analysis requires you to break down the question into different parts, i.e., to *separate out different strands of an argument or offer more than one argument*. The structured worksheets suggest evaluation points; the APFCCs should provide the much needed psychological evidence as your answer must be informed (backed up by psychological research) and not just an opinion. The appendix on 'How to impress the examiner on AO2' suggests methodological criticisms, providing examples from different topic areas to develop this skill and offers further advice on essay writing.

Of course, answering the question involves more than this, which is why one model answer per topic has been included to illustrate how to relate the answer to the question, i.e., make effective use of material, offer commentary, and draw conclusions throughout the answer.

Ψ Model answers

These demonstrate how to approach the essay question. The model answers are restricted to the critical issues whereas of course the essay question can be drawn from any part of the Specification. Although all the possible questions have not been covered, noting the approach taken in the examples will help you develop excellent AO2 skills, which you can then transfer to any AO2 question. See the essay plans for all possible questions, and the 'Step-by-step guide to answering exam questions' for more information on essay technique.

AO3 tests design, implementation, and reporting of psychological research

Ψ Research methods, Unit 3

The assessment objective AO3 will be examined via the research methods question. The 'Research methods revision' summary will fully prepare you to achieve well on this assessment objective.

QoWC (quality of written communication)

There are 2 marks per unit paper for good use of grammar and punctuation, correct spelling, legible handwriting, clear expression, and accurate use of technical terms. This should pose few problems for an AS level student!

Step-by-step Guide to Answering Exam Questions

Cross-reference this with the Specification, the AO1 revision summaries, the 'Using this in the exam' sections on the worksheets, and see 'Examination skills' for further information on the types of exam question.

There are three exam papers:

PYA1: Human Memory and Attachments in Development
PYA2: Stress and Abnormality
PYA3: Social Influence and Research Methods

You must answer one question per topic (memory, attachments, etc.), and so two questions per paper. You have a choice between two questions on all topics apart from Research Methods. All questions total 30 marks and there is 1 further mark for quality of written communication per question and so 2 marks per paper. For all questions bar those on research methods, parts (a) and (b) are AO1 questions and total 12 marks, and part (c) is the 18-mark essay question, made up of 6 AO1 marks and 12 AO2 marks. The one Research Methods question includes AO1 (3 marks), AO2 (6 marks), and AO3 (21 marks).

The following step-by-step guide will help you to perform well in the exams:

1. **Read the questions carefully**. So, nothing difficult there! But you must read and decide which of the two questions you will answer quickly. The best way to do this is to read the essay questions first and let this determine your choice, as the essay constitutes nearly two-thirds of the marks. So please don't start with an AO1 question and then decide you don't like the look of the essay in that question. There isn't time in half an hour to switch questions. Although some students report doing just this, it really isn't advisable. Also, if you are asked to outline/describe do not include criticisms, and if asked to give criticisms do not describe.

2. **Read through all the questions before answering them**. This is because two sub-parts may be linked, and this is particularly likely on Research Methods. For example, one sub-part may ask you to describe how you would gain a sample for a study and then the next sub-part may ask you to evaluate the method. Thus, you need to choose a sampling method that will provide enough content for the next sub-part. Or you could be asked to identify a source of bias and then explain how you would control it, so of course you need to select something that you know how to control.

3. **Relate your answer to the question**. Research Methods questions frequently include the phrase 'in the context of this investigation', which means you must relate your answer explicitly to the study described in the question. For example, if you are asked to give an advantage of a research method then you must explain why the research method is advantageous for the study described in the question rather than just giving an advantage of using that research method in general. Or you could be asked to identify criticisms of a theory or research, so don't make generalised criticisms but relate them to the theory/research that is being discussed, e.g., if asked to identify ethical issues in a social influence question, don't just describe the issues but explain them in relation to the study or studies being considered.

4. **Use the mark allocation**. The length of your answer must be in proportion to the marks available, so make sure that you are aware of the number of marks on offer so you can give an appropriate amount of detail. Don't write too little (one sentence for a 3-mark answer is likely to fall below 'pass standard') and don't write too much. Particularly watch out for writing too much, as this will penalise your ability to answer later questions as there is simply not enough time for writing extra material, i.e., do not spend 10 minutes on a 6-mark question as you will lose out elsewhere.

5. **Watch the time**. You only have 1 minute per mark, so try not to go over this.

6. **Label your answers**. The examiner should have no difficulty working out which question you have answered, so it must be numbered clearly, e.g., Q1 (a), (b), (c). Also, if two explanations, factors, or criticisms are asked for number these i) and ii). Do not leave it to the examiner to work out which is point one and which is point two—you want them to be in a good mood!

7. **Read through your answers**. Do this if you are sitting waiting for the exam to end, which is unlikely to happen given the tight time limits. But if you do have some spare time, check for spelling and grammar as you can lose marks on this; 2 marks per paper. Also check for the accuracy of your answers and see if there is anything else you could possibly add in.

8. **Identify which parts are required in the APFCC questions**. Once these parts have been identified, label them, e.g., aims, procedures, findings, conclusions, criticisms. This should help you to avoid giving irrelevant content such as giving the aim when the procedures and findings have been asked for, and do double-check that you haven't referred to the wrong part of the study. Make sure that you can distinguish findings (fact) from conclusions (opinion); see the findings and conclusions parts of the APFCC worksheets for more information. Make sure you are able to supplement the findings and conclusions from the APFCC with other research if necessary so that you have enough content for 6 marks. Also, note that the conclusions should answer the aims.

9. **Highlight important phrases in the stimulus material**. This particularly applies to Research Methods but may also be relevant to the quote in the essay questions. For example, highlight the method in the Research Methods question stimulus. This will hopefully help you to avoid the easy mistake of referring to the research method as an experiment when a non-experimental method has been used. In fact, it might be best if you refer to the research in the question stimulus as 'the study' to avoid this pitfall. Here are some important things to look for in the Research Methods question stimulus:

   - The type of method—Is it an experiment, correlation, interview, questionnaire, or naturalistic observation?

   - The hypothesis—Is it experimental or correlational and hence should you use the word 'difference' or 'correlation' if asked to state the hypothesis? Is the hypothesis directional or non-directional?

   - The research design—Is the design experimental or non-experimental? Try to identify any design features, e.g., the materials, pilot study, controls.

   - The experimental design—Are the participants in one condition (independent measures) or two (repeated measures)?

   - The sample method—Did the experimenters advertise for participants? Or select them randomly? Or just take whoever was available, i.e., opportunity sampling?

   - Controls of bias and confounding variables—Have any of the following been considered: standardisation, counterbalancing, random allocation, single- and double-blind designs?

10. **Essay technique**. The following points will hopefully assist you with writing essays.

    i) **Structure**—The three-paragraph model with a conclusion is a useful way to achieve structure and get the correct ratio of one-third AO1:two-thirds AO2, as the first paragraph can be AO1 and the next two paragraphs AO2. Aim to write in total 300+ words with approximately 100–120 words per paragraph. Try to write about something different in each paragraph, e.g., a different argument for or against, so that your answer has breadth. So a formula for essay writing could be this:

    Paragraph 1: AO1 100–120 words, approximate time 5 minutes and must aim for 6 marks.

    Show you understand the question by defining terms and identifying the main features of whatever the question has asked you to consider. Don't begin with a description of lots of studies as this often results in a mainly AO1 answer, so save the research for AO2.

    Paragraph 2: AO2 100–120 words, approximate time 5 minutes and must aim for 6 marks.

    Research evidence in support (make sure you use link phrases like this), i.e., the arguments for and/or positive criticisms; the 'pros'.

    Paragraph 3: AO2 100–120 words, approximate time 5 minutes and must aim for 6 marks.

    Research evidence that contradicts/challenges, i.e., the arguments against and/or negative criticisms; the 'cons'.

    Make sure that any research you cite in paragraphs 2 and 3 is phrased as AO2, e.g., 'this research suggests…' or 'because the findings show…'. Avoid description by limiting content on research evidence to findings/conclusions, and give your own conclusions to keep your answer evaluative. Then criticise the research evidence including positive and negative criticisms. Remember that if you question the validity you are also questioning the truth, which reduces the value of the research. Validity is crucial in weighing up the evidence for and against an argument, and assessing research contributions.

Conclusion: Weigh up strengths and weaknesses, and assess explanatory power, i.e., insights offered, and 'to what extent', if this has been asked in the question. You may find it useful to plan your conclusion first and then organise your essay to work towards this.

This is a useful framework but you don't have to be as prescriptive as this; note how some of the model essays take this structure but others vary slightly. Try to see the essay question as something a friend has just asked your advice about. To begin with you need to offer some knowledge and understanding (AO1) but not too much to bore them senseless! Next you need to consider both sides of the argument, i.e., debate the pros and cons, and then give your conclusion.

ii) **Selective use of material**—Don't write everything you know about a subject, and certainly don't describe too much, as the majority of marks are AO2. Hence, you must select the most relevant material. This is something you need to practise before the exam and you can do this when you prepare model answers. There are 4 marks available for effective use of material.

iii) **Evaluation and analysis**—AO2 is allocated 12 marks in the 18-mark question. Hence, two-thirds of the content must be evaluation and analysis. You can use the evaluation you have practised in the appendix 'How to impress the examiner on AO2' to weigh up the strengths and weaknesses of psychological theory and research. Analysis requires you to break down the question, which can be done by looking at the arguments for and against whatever the question is suggesting. There are 4 marks available for thorough analysis.

iv) **Psychologically informed**—Whilst you may well have your own opinion in answer to the question it is vital that you back this up with psychological research and theory as there are 4 marks available for how informed your answer is. This is true of any exam question, be it AO1 or essay; you need to refer to psychological research/theory so that your answer is more than 'the man on the street answer'! You can use this to support or contradict the argument you are making. Use the APFCCs and the research you write about on the worksheets to make your answer informed, so it is *essential* that you include link sentences here, e.g., 'this research supports/contradicts/illustrates…', to make your content evaluative rather than merely descriptive. The research evidence is a good source of AO2 if presented correctly.

v) **Description**—There are 6 AO1 marks, 3 for accuracy and 3 for the amount of detail. A good way to start your answer is to define terms in the question, showing that you understand the question. Thus, your first paragraph will be descriptive and this will ensure that one-third of your answer can access the 6 AO1 marks that are available. After this you must refer to research (theory and/or studies) *without* describing it; use it solely as evaluation by using the link sentences suggested above.

vi) **Does your answer have merit?**—Consider the folllowing points in order to determine this:

Methodological criticisms—Criticise the research method and assess what that means in terms of the validity of the research. Usually this means the research lacks validity (internal and/or external), which reduces the meaningfulness of the findings and the strength of the argument that has been used to support/contradict.

Ethical criticisms—Do the ends justify the means? Are the findings socially sensitive?

Real-life validity, i.e., explanatory power, applications, contextualise—Does the research/theory work in real life and so have value, truth, and validity? Research that lacks internal validity is unlikely to generalise to real life, which means it lacks ecological validity (a form of external validity). Consider the benefits (applications) of the research. Consider the extent to which the research is dated because it is a product of the time and context (historical, political, social, and cultural) when it was conducted and so lacks external validity (temporal, ecological, and population validity) to the current context.

Individual, social, and cultural diversity—Consider if these are accounted for. Or do participant variables/individual differences limit the generalisability of the research?

Theoretical criticisms—Consider reductionism and determinism, and nature/nurture.

Practice, practice, practice… and more practice—Remember the 18-mark question is supposed to be a mini-essay rather than a shopping list so do not just list criticisms.

APFCC Template

APFCC stands for AIMS, PROCEDURES, FINDINGS (results), CONCLUSIONS, and CRITICISMS (evaluation). Exam questions (AO1 requirement) will be based on the APFCCs and so they are key revision aids. The template provides a guide to the details you should try to include. However, if some of the details are not available in your textbook do not worry, simply fill in as much as you can. Try to refer to this when you are filling in the APFCCs for each topic area. There are 16 research areas that you need to illustrate with a study. You do not need to use the ones suggested on the APFCCs but do make sure you have covered all 16 research areas. See the appendix of Brody and Dwyer's *Revise Psychology for AS Level* (pages 179–192) for a full set of completed APFCCs. Also complete the 'Findings/conclusions' worksheets in the appendices section of this book.

EXAM TIP: You may be asked to evaluate (criticise) the study you have described. Note the mnemonic MET! Prepare two criticisms for each study and make sure each criticism is worth 3 marks. So don't just state, elaborate! For example, don't just say a study has low ecological validity but explain why and make sure you fully relate the criticism to the research.

Aims:	What did the research hope to discover? Was this based on past research/psychological theory? Does the research aim to support a particular theory?
Procedures:	How was the research carried out? Pre-test (if relevant).
Sample:	Type (e.g., random, opportunity), size, and relevant characteristics (e.g., student sample, Western sample).
Research method:	Experimental or non-experimental and design (e.g., independent or repeated measures, matched participants, or correlational). Explain how the data were collected. How were the variables measured (e.g., questionnaire using rating scales)? Were any attempts made to control confounding/extraneous variables?
Materials:	Questionnaire, interview schedule, observation criteria, test materials, etc.
Findings:	Explain the results. What did the researchers discover? Include any descriptive statistics if they are given, e.g., percentages.
Conclusions:	What understanding/insight does the research yield? What are the implications of the research? Can any conclusive findings be inferred (e.g., 'the research showed that…')?
Criticisms:	What are the strengths and weaknesses? Criticisms can be positive and negative.
MET:	**M**ethodological—Generalisability, validity, reliability, causation, strengths and weaknesses of the method, quantitative vs. qualitative approach. **E**thical—Have ethical guidelines been broken and if so can this be justified? Is the research socially sensitive? **T**heoretical—Physiological vs. psychological perspectives, reductionism, biological/environmental determinism, descriptive vs. explanatory.
Note: Many criticisms are possible but you only ever need two at most.	

Human Memory Learning Objectives

On completion of this topic you should be familiar with the following.

Short-term memory and long-term memory

- Define memory, short-term memory (STM), and long-term memory (LTM).
- Distinguish between STM and LTM in terms of encoding, capacity, and duration and be able to define these terms.
- Describe the Aims, Procedures, Findings, Conclusions, Criticisms (APFCC) for a study into the nature of STM, e.g., 'the Brown–Peterson technique' for the duration of STM (Peterson & Peterson, 1959), and a study into the nature of LTM, e.g., 'classmates are never forgotten' for the duration of LTM (Bahrick et al., 1975).
- Define, describe, and evaluate the models of memory: the multi-store model and either the levels of processing model or the working memory model.

Forgetting

- Define forgetting, flashbulb memory, and repression.
- Outline and evaluate the explanations of forgetting in STM, which include trace decay and displacement, and in LTM, which include trace decay, interference, cue dependent, and repression. Relate these explanations to the issues of AVAILABILITY and ACCESSIBILITY.
- Describe and evaluate emotional factors in forgetting, including flashbulb memories and repression.

Critical issue—Eyewitness testimony

- Define and describe reconstructive memory and eyewitness testimony.
- Assess the practical applications of memory research into eyewitness testimony, which includes reconstructive memory and Loftus' research on leading questions.

Cross-reference the above learning objectives with the Specification and fill in the self-assessment box below on completion of the topic.

SELF-ASSESSMENT BOX

☺ **Which of the above do you know?**

☹ **Are there any gaps in your knowledge that need to be targeted during revision?**

STM and LTM

For details, see Eysenck's textbook (page 41) and Brody and Dwyer's revision guide (page 20). Use the cues in the tables to guide your note taking and fill in the gaps using the letter clues provided.

Definition of memory

The nature of memory definitions		
Encoding	**Capacity**	**Duration**

Two types of memory have been identified; s_____-term memory (STM) and l___-term memory (LTM) and these are generally considered to be memory structures or stores of information.

STM: This is our present conscious experience where information is processed through attention and rehearsal. Hence, it is also called working memory. Information is s_____ temporarily and it is thought to have limited c_____ and d_____.

LTM: Information can be stored p_____, for example, people can remember childhood memories in old age. It is thought to have u_____ capacity and duration if information has been processed sufficiently. The complexity and variety of LTM has led to different types of memory being identified, e.g., d_____ (memory for facts) and p_____ (memory for skills).

To use a computer analogy, STM is the RAM and LTM is the ROM.

The structure of memory definitions	
Short-term memory	**Long-term memory**

Store	Encoding	Capacity	Duration
STM			
LTM			
Differences between STM and LTM			

Using this in the exam

AO1 questions:

Explain what is meant by the terms short-term memory and long-term memory. (3 + 3 marks)
Only two definitions (3 + 3 marks) or three definitions (2 + 2 + 2 marks) will be asked for in any one question and the terms can be drawn from any of the memory key terms; see the complete list on the 'Human memory revision AO1' summary.
Describe the APFCC for a study into the nature of STM. (6 marks)
Describe the APFCC for a study into the nature of LTM. (6 marks)
APFCC questions are always worth 6 marks.
Describe the findings (or conclusions) of research into STM/LTM. (6 marks)
Describe two/three differences between short-term and long-term memory. (3 + 3 marks/2 + 2 + 2 marks)
Outline the differences between short-term and long-term memory. (6 marks)
In other words, encoding, capacity, and duration.
Outline two factors that influence encoding, capacity, and duration of STM and LTM. (3 + 3 marks)
The nature of the information and which store (STM/LTM) both influence encoding, capacity, and duration.

Essay question:

To what extent does research evidence (theory and/or studies) support the view that
short-term and long-term memory are separate stores? (18 marks)

Models of Memory

For details, see Eysenck's textbook (page 42) and Brody and Dwyer's revision guide (page 21). Use the cues in the tables to guide your note taking.

Multi-store model—Atkinson and Shiffrin (1968)

Description

Fill in the gaps using your textbook and the letter clues provided.

According to this model there are three memory stores. Information enters s_____y m_____y and if attended to enters   S____. M_____e r_____l refers to how the information is maintained in STM. It is transferred to LTM through el_____ r_____ (verbal repetition). Without r_____ it is l____. The more something is r_____ the stronger the m_____ trace. This model emphasises st_____ (the three stores) and pr_____ (attention and rehearsal).

Positive evaluation

Research evidence to support the theory:

Ψ Differences in encoding, capacity, and duration between STM and LTM. Refer to the APFCC studies.

Ψ Primacy and recency effects. See Glanzer and Cunitz's (1966) research.

Ψ Case studies of brain damaged patients, e.g., KF and HM.

Negative evaluation

Ψ Rehearsal is not essential for the transfer of information into LTM and the emphasis placed on this may be a consequence of the artificiality of memory experiments. See Hyde and Jenkins' (1973) study of incidental learning. Consider flashbulb memory.

Ψ STM and LTM are not single stores and it is questionable whether they are separate stores.

Ψ It is an active not a passive process (see the working memory model, which does consider STM to be an active processor); a two-way not one-way transfer of information.

Ψ Are STM and LTM separate stores?

You can also use the next two models (levels of processing and working memory) to evaluate the multi-store model. Cover both of these as you must know at least one alternative to the multi-store model, according to the Specification.

Levels of processing model—Craik and Lockhart (1972)

Description

Fill in the gaps using your textbook and the letter clues provided.

The levels of processing model expands upon the multi-store model's simplistic account of the transfer of information between STM and LTM. R_____ alone is not enough to account for m_____. It is the d_____ of processing that determines whether information is s_____ over long periods. R_____ is one form of processing, but there are other deeper forms such as d_____ of analysis, e_____, o_____, and d_____. M_____ is a by-product of this m_____l p_____g.

Positive evaluation

Research evidence to support the theory:

Ψ Craik and Tulving's (1975) depth of processing study.

Follow-up research that extended the concept of depth of processing:

Ψ Craik and Tulving's (1975) study on elaboration.

Ψ Mandler's (1967) study of organisation.

Ψ Eysenck and Eysenck's (1980) study of distinctiveness.

Ψ Personal relevance, e.g., a humorous anecdote may be remembered with no rehearsal.

Negative evaluation

Ψ Circular argument because depth of processing cannot be measured.

Ψ Level of processing may not be isolated, i.e., it is not clear if processing is taking place at just the level prescribed or if other forms are also being used.

Ψ Conflicting research evidence (Morris, Bransford, & Franks, 1977).

Ψ Descriptive rather than explanatory as it does not explain why deep processing is better.

Ψ May confuse effort with depth.

Working memory model—Baddeley and Hitch (1974)

Description

Fill in the gaps using your textbook and the letter clues provided.

This expands on the multi-store model's over-simplistic representation of STM as a s_____ store. According to the working memory model, STM is an active store made up of three components. It consists of the a_____-p_____ l____ for acoustic memories, the v_____-s_____ s_____ p___ for visual memories, and the c_____ e_____ controls the different slave systems and attention.

Positive evaluation

Research evidence to support the theory:

Ψ Hitch and Baddeley (1976) and the dual-task technique.

Ψ Baddeley and Lewis (1981).

Ψ The concept of working memory as an active processor is an advance over the multi-store's representation of STM as a passive store and has validity because the model can account for real-life activities such as reading and arithmetic.

Ψ It is a more realistic account of verbal rehearsal.

Negative evaluation

Ψ We still lack an understanding of key concepts, e.g., the central executive.

Ψ Oversimplified view of STM to see it as under the control of one mechanism, the central executive.

Using this in the exam

AO1 questions:

Explain what is meant by the term multi-store model. (6 marks)

Explain the main features of the multi-store model OR one alternative to the multi-store model. (6 marks)

Give two criticisms of the multi-store model OR one alternative to the multi-store model. (3 + 3 marks)/(6 marks)

Essay questions:

Consider the extent to which criticisms of the multi-store model are supported by psychological research (theories and/or studies). (18 marks)

Outline and evaluate the multi-store model of memory OR one alternative model to the multi-store model (e.g., levels of processing or working memory). (18 marks)

Forgetting

For details, see Eysenck's textbook (page 63) and Brody and Dwyer's revision guide (page 27). Use the cues in the table to guide your note taking and fill in the gaps using the letter clues provided.

Definition of forgetting

Forgetting occurs due to a problem in processing (i.e., encoding, storage, and retrieval): Fill in the gaps with 'availability' or 'accessibility' as appropriate.

Ψ Encoding and storage problems lead to the issue of a_____. Information may have disappeared from memory and so is not available to recall, as would occur with trace decay and displacement/interference.

Ψ Retrieval problems lead to the issue of a_____. Information is in memory but it cannot be found. A prompt or cue is needed to make it accessible.

Forgetting in STM is due to a lack of a_____, as STM is a limited capacity store. Forgetting in LTM could be due to a lack of availability or accessibility. However, as LTM has an infinite capacity and duration, forgetting is more likely to be due to a lack of a_____.

Forgetting in STM	
Trace decay	**Displacement**
Ψ The physical trace disappears, i.e., physical decay.	Ψ The last one in pushes the first out.
Ψ Research evidence (Peterson & Peterson, 1959).	Ψ Research evidence—the serial probe technique (Waugh & Norman, 1965).
Evaluation	**Evaluation**
Ψ Decay or displacement?	Ψ Displacement or decay?

Forgetting in LTM

Availability	Accessibility
Trace decay Ψ The physical trace disappears, i.e., physical decay. Ψ Research evidence (Jenkins & Dallenbach, 1924). **Evaluation** Ψ Interference or decay? Ψ Methodological criticisms.	**Cue-dependent forgetting/retrieval failure, e.g., the 'tip-of-the-tongue' phenomenon** Ψ Cues reverse the effect of interference. Ψ Research evidence (Tulving & Psotka, 1971). Ψ Encoding specificity principle. Ψ Cue-dependent forgetting, i.e., retrieval failure (context- and state-dependent).
Interference Ψ Proactive interference. Ψ Retroactive interference. **Evaluation** Ψ Lacks mundane realism. Why? Ψ The effect is reversed through cued recall (Tulving & Psotka, 1971).	**Evaluation** Ψ Cue-dependent forgetting is considered to be the main explanation for forgetting. Ψ Low mundane realism that may limit generalisability to everyday memory.

Using this in the exam

AO1 questions:

Outline two explanations of forgetting in memory.   (3 + 3 marks)
You can choose any two explanations of forgetting in STM or LTM, or the question may specify STM or LTM.
Outline two factors that influence forgetting in STM or LTM.   (3 + 3 marks)

Essay questions:

Outline and consider the strengths and weaknesses of explanations of forgetting in memory.   (18 marks)
Outline and evaluate two or more explanations of forgetting in <u>long-term memory OR short-term memory</u>, OR Consider the strengths and weaknesses of explanations of forgetting in <u>long-term memory OR short-term memory</u>.   (18 marks)

Emotional Factors in Forgetting

We remember more when we are happy due to:

- State-dependent memory.
- Flashbulb memory.

For details, see Eysenck's textbook (page 70) and Brody and Dwyer's revision guide (page 28). Fill in the gaps using the letter clues provided and use the cues in the table to guide your note taking.

Emotions affect cognitive processing. High e_____ arousal can inhibit or enhance m_____ depending on the nature of the memory content. For example, if the memory causes anxiety it may be r_____. Alternatively, evidence suggests that whilst high a_____ may inhibit recall initially it can increase recall in the long term (Levinger & Clark, 1961). F_____ memories of important and emotionally significant events are memorable because of high emotional arousal.

Repression (motivated forgetting)
Definition of repression
Ψ Ego defence (Freud, 1915).
Ψ Evidence for repression.
Ψ Recovered memories of sexual abuse. Which syndrome is associated with these?
Evaluation Ψ Emotional arousal can improve recall, e.g., flashbulb memory. Ψ Methodological and ethical criticisms of the research.

Flashbulb memory

Definition of flashbulb memory

Ψ Examples of flashbulb memories.

9/11

Ψ What causes a flashbulb memory? Is it a biological mechanism (Cahill & McGaugh, 1998)?

Evaluation

Ψ Are flashbulb memories accurate? How does a lack of reliability (consistency) bring into question the validity of flashbulb memory?

Ψ Methodological criticisms of the research. How does rehearsal challenge the validity of flashbulb memory?

Ψ Emotion may inhibit rather than enhance memory.

Using this in the exam

AO1 questions:

Explain what is meant by the terms repression and flashbulb memory. (3 + 3 marks)
Outline two emotional factors that influence memory. (3 + 3 marks)

Essay questions:

Outline and evaluate psychological research (theories and/or studies) into the role of repression in forgetting. (18 marks)
Outline and evaluate psychological research (theories and/or studies) into flashbulb memory. (18 marks)
Consider what psychological research (theories and/or studies) has told us about the role of emotional factors in forgetting. (18 marks)

Reconstructive Memory

For details, see Eysenck's textbook (page 75) and Brody and Dwyer's revision guide (page 32). Fill in the gaps using the letter clues provided and use the cues in the table to guide your note taking.

Reconstruction is the a_____ process used to r_____ memories as people do not have total recall. R_____ consist of real elements of a memory and g____ in memory that people fill in based on their knowledge of the world (called s_____). Thus, schemas lead to d_____ and this explains why eyewitness testimony (EWT) is u_____. To use a jigsaw as an analogy, some bits are 'real' pieces and some bits are 'made-up', which does not provide an accurate picture of the witnessed event.

You could also be asked an APFCC question on this so please complete the Bartlett (1932) APFCC.

Definition of reconstructive memory

Bartlett's (1932) repeated reproduction method— 'The War of the Ghosts'

Ψ Why was the story from an unfamiliar culture?

Ψ What distortions were evident in the reconstructions?

Evaluation

Ψ The research lacked objectivity, which means it may be subject to researcher bias and other factors may have affected memory.

Ψ High ecological validity as the task is generalisable to everyday memory demands.

Schema theory

Ψ A schema is an organised package of information that stores knowledge about the world.

Ψ People have similar schemas, e.g., stereotypes (Allport & Postman, 1947).

Ψ The influence of schemas on learning and recall.

Evaluation

Ψ Schema theory does explain how data is stored and retrieved.

Ψ Schema theory may overemphasise the inaccuracy of memory.

Using this in the exam

AO1 questions:

Explain what is meant by the terms reconstructive memory and repression.   (3 + 3 marks)
Describe the APFCC for one study that has investigated reconstructive memory.   (6 marks)
Outline two factors that influence reconstructive memory.   (3 + 3 marks)
Give two criticisms of reconstructive memory as an explanation of forgetting.   (3 + 3 marks)

Essay question:

Outline and evaluate the insights provided by psychological research (theories and/or studies)
into reconstructive memory.   (18 marks)

Eyewitness Testimony

For details, see Eysenck's textbook (page 74) and Brody and Dwyer's revision guide (page 32). Fill in the gaps using the letter clues and use the cues in the table to guide your note taking.

Eyewitness testimony (EWT) is a major application of our knowledge of m_____. EWT is likely to rely on r_____ memory and the worksheet on this explains why reconstruction d_____ the reliability of EWT. The evidence for the u_____ of EWT is considerable. For example, the Devlin report (1976) advised that convictions should not be based on EWT alone. However, EWT remains an issue because j_____ are highly influenced by it. Reconstruction is not the only source of distortion in EWT; the language used, in particular l_____ q_____, can b____ EWT.

You could also be asked an APFCC question on this so please complete the Loftus and Palmer (1974) APFCC.

Definition of eyewitness testimony (EWT)
Witnesses do an event would be asked to recall what they had seen. Remembering an event in detail, given as witness, are asked to give evidence in court.

The effect of language on recall	
Leading questions (cross-reference with APFCC on EWT) *Loftus & Palmer* *Participants shown a video of a car crash. Then asked 'how fast do you think the cars were going when they smashed into each other' rephrased. Those asked the 'smashed' question thought the cars were going significantly faster than those asked the 'smashed' question.*	**Evaluation** Ψ Demand characteristics mean internal validity must be questioned. *The following is may*
Post-event information—'a' vs. 'the' (Loftus & Zanni, 1975)	Ψ Artificiality means external validity is low and so may not generalise to real-life EWT. Yuille and Cutshall (1986) found much higher accuracy and reliability in real-life EWT.
Memory blending	

Other factors that influence the accuracy of EWT

Witness factors—characteristics	Event factors—to do with the situation
Ψ Arousal of the witness.	Ψ Exposure time.
Ψ Cultural stereotypes of the witness.	Ψ Weapon focus.
Ψ Familiarity/knowledge of suspect helps with face recognition.	Ψ Time between event and recording of the EWT.

Positive applications of the research that have improved the accuracy of EWT

Implications for police procedures

Ψ Improvements in interview techniques were suggested in Home Office guidelines.

The basic cognitive interview (Geiselman et al., 1985)

The enhanced interview

Assess the reliability and accuracy of EWT

Research suggests that the language used can d_____ the information that is stored and retrieved; that is, l_____ q_____ can bias EWT. Leading questions can have a suggestibility effect as they can falsely suggest information. This supports Bartlett's (1932) re_____ approach to memory as the research on EWT suggests that EWT involves active reconstruction, where prior knowledge (s_____) can lead to memory distortions at storage and retrieval. Also post-event i_____ and memory b_____ may further distort information. However, the research evidence is based on l_____ e_____ and it may well be the case that real-life EWT is much more a_____ than these would suggest.

Using this in the exam

AO1 questions:

Explain what is mean by the terms eyewitness testimony and reconstructive memory.	(3 + 3 marks)
Describe the APFCC for one study that has investigated the accuracy of eyewitness testimony.	(6 marks)
Outline the findings (or conclusions) of research into eyewitness testimony.	(6 marks)
Describe two factors that influence the accuracy of eyewitness testimony.	(3 + 3 marks)

Essay questions:

Consider what psychological research (theories and/or studies) has told us about the accuracy of eyewitness testimony.	(18 marks)
Consider the extent to which research into memory has helped our understanding of eyewitness testimony.	(18 marks)
Consider what psychological research (theories and/or studies) has told us about how to improve the accuracy of eyewitness testimony.	(18 marks)

Human Memory APFCCs

EXAM TIP: You have to be able to describe the APFCC for studies on the nature of STM, the nature of LTM, reconstructive memory, and the role of leading questions in EWT. But you may be asked a general question on the findings or conclusions of research into any of the above. So make sure you know the findings or conclusions in sufficient detail for 6 marks. Cross-reference with the completed APFCCs in the appendix of the Brody and Dwyer revision guide (pages 179–182).

Study into the nature of STM e.g., 'the Brown–Peterson technique' (Peterson & Peterson, 1959)

Aims: To test the duration of STM and to discover whether rehearsal plays an important part in storing information in ST.

Procedures: A number of participants were asked to learn a set of trigrams. Once they had remembered them they were asked to count backwards from a different number in threes (data was gathered)

Findings: They found that the longer participants waited without rehearsing the less recollections were able to do.

Conclusions: Rehearsal allows for chunks of information to be stored in STM and then passed onto LTM.

Criticisms:

Study into the nature of LTM e.g., 'classmates are never forgotten' (Bahrick et al., 1975)

Aims:

Procedures:

Findings:

Conclusions:

Criticisms:

Study of reconstructive memory—'The War of the Ghosts' (Bartlett, 1932)

Aims:

Procedures:

Findings:

Conclusions:

Criticisms:

Study of leading questions in EWT
(Loftus & Palmer, 1974)

Aims:

To discover whether _____ questions can affect _____ answers that a witness gave _____ _____ it can _____ _____ the answers given.

Procedures:

Participants _____ _____ _____ _____ _____ _____ _____ _____ _____ _____ the cars _____ _____ _____ _____ other _____ _____ asked _____ _____ _____ _____ _____ _____ each other _____ _____ _____

Findings:

The ones who were asked _____ _____ _____ _____ the cars were going _____ _____ _____ _____ _____ _____ _____ leading question.
_____ _____ _____ _____ _____ _____ _____ who were asked the smashed question.

Conclusions:

Criticisms:

Human Memory Revision AO1

Use this as a checklist, i.e., tick off when you feel confident you can answer the following questions and/or have prepared a model answer for each type of question. The range of potential exam questions is finite so you can prepare for all possibilities.

Definition questions (2 + 2 + 2 marks or 3 + 3 marks)

You may be asked to define any of the terms that appear on the Specification, except for those that are given as examples. So cross-reference with the Specification.

> **EXAM TIP**: If you have not included enough content to access all of the marks, give an example.

Memory	Short-term memory	Long-term memory
Multi-store model	Forgetting	Repression
Flashbulb memory	Reconstructive memory	Eyewitness testimony
Leading questions		

Definitions

Cross-reference with the glossary in the Brody and Dwyer revision guide (pages 193–202).

Example exam question: What is meant by the terms… *[and two or three of the following would be stated]*

Memory:

Short-term memory:

Long-term memory:

Multi-store model:

Forgetting:

Repression:

Flashbulb memory:

Reconstructive memory:

Eyewitness testimony:

Leading questions:

Research questions (6 marks or 3 + 3 marks)

Cross-reference with the completed APFCCs in the appendix of the Brody and Dwyer revision guide (pages 179–182).

Example exam questions: Describe the aims/procedures/findings/conclusions/one criticism of a study into... *[any two aspects could be specified]* (6 marks)

Describe the findings of research into... (6 marks)

Describe the conclusions of research into... (6 marks)

Give two criticisms of research into... (3 + 3 marks)

> **EXAM TIP**: The question may ask for any two APFCCs or may just ask for the *findings*, *conclusions*, or *two criticisms*. So be prepared to give enough detail for 6 marks on the findings or conclusions and know two criticisms for all studies in sufficient detail for 3 marks each.

Make sure you can give the APFCCs for the following human memory studies:

Q: Outline the APFCC of one study into the nature of short-term memory. OR findings/conclusions.
A: Peterson and Peterson's (1959) 'Brown–Peterson technique' for the duration of STM, and Glanzer and Cunitz (1966) if findings/conclusions.

Q: Outline the APFCC of one study into the nature of long-term memory.
A: Bahrick et al.'s (1976) 'classmates are never forgotten' for the duration of LTM, and Cohen and Squire (1980) about the different types of LTM if findings/conclusions.

Q: Outline the APFCC of one study of reconstructive memory. OR findings/conclusions.
A: Bartlett's (1932) 'The War of the Ghosts' research, and Sulin and Dooling (1974) if findings/conclusions.

Q: Outline the APFCC of one study of eyewitness testimony. OR findings/conclusions.
A: Loftus and Palmer's (1974) study on leading questions, and Loftus' follow-up research if findings/conclusions.

These are only suggestions, so use other studies if you prefer.

Explanations/theories questions (6 marks or 3 + 3 marks)

These questions could be worded in a number of ways.

Example exam questions: Describe one explanation of... (6 marks)
Outline two explanations of... (3 + 3 marks)
Outline one explanation and give one criticism of... (3 + 3 marks)
Outline the main features of... (6 marks)
Outline two factors that explain... (3 + 3 marks)
Outline two factors that influence... (3 + 3 marks)
Outline two ways that... (3 + 3 marks)
Outline two effects of... (3 + 3 marks)

Q: Outline two factors that influence encoding in memory. *[STM or LTM could be specified.]*

A: Attention, the nature of the material being encoded (e.g., visual or auditory stimuli), and the memory store that the material is being encoded into, i.e., STM or LTM. See 'STM and LTM'.

Q: Outline two factors that influence the capacity of memory. *[STM or LTM could be specified.]*

A: Chunking, the nature of the material (e.g., letters or numbers) and the memory store, i.e., STM or LTM. See 'STM and LTM'.

Q: Outline two factors that influence the duration of memory. *[STM or LTM could be specified.]*

A: Rehearsal, the nature of the material (e.g., whether it is personally relevant or a word list), and the memory store, i.e., STM and LTM. The explanations of forgetting could be used to explain a lack of duration, or reconstruction to explain why the memory that endures may be inaccurate. See 'STM and LTM', 'Forgetting', and 'Reconstructive memory'.

Q: Outline two factors that influence STM.

A: Rehearsal as proposed by the multi-store model and attention as proposed by the working memory model; see 'Models of memory'. Or even trace decay, displacement, and emotional factors; see 'Forgetting' and 'Emotional factors in forgetting'.

Q: Outline two factors that influence LTM.

A: Rehearsal as proposed by the multi-store model and level of processing as detailed by that model. Or interference, cued-retrieval, repression, flashbulb memory, reconstruction; see 'Models of memory', 'Forgetting', 'Emotional factors in forgetting', and 'Reconstructive memory'.

Q: Outline the main features of the multi-store model OR an alternative to the multi-store model. OR Outline and give one criticism...

A: Describe the structure and/or processes of the relevant model. You may find it useful to include a diagram in your answer, but only as a part of your answer, i.e., it must be in addition to the written description. See 'Models of memory' and criticisms answers.

Q: Outline two explanations of forgetting in STM. OR Explain two factors that influence forgetting in STM. OR Describe one theory of forgetting in STM. OR Outline one explanation of forgetting in STM and give one criticism.

A: Trace decay and displacement. See 'Forgetting' and criticisms answers.

Q: Outline two explanations of forgetting in LTM. OR Explain two factors that influence forgetting in LTM. OR Describe one theory of forgetting in LTM. OR Outline one explanation of forgetting in LTM and give one criticism.

A: Interference and cue-dependent forgetting (retrieval-failure). See 'Forgetting' and criticisms answers.

Q: Outline the emotional factors in forgetting. OR Explain two emotional factors that influence forgetting. OR Outline one emotional factor and give one criticism.

A: Repression, flashbulb memory, and state-dependent memory. See 'Emotional factors in forgetting', and the criticisms answers.

Q: Outline two factors that influence flashbulb memory. OR Outline one explanation of flashbulb memory.

A: High emotional arousal and personal/cultural relevance of the event and for the explanation outline the biological mechanism explanation for flashbulb memory. See 'Emotional factors in forgetting'.

Q: Outline two factors that influence repression.

A: Emotional arousal as measured by the galvanic skin response and past experience of traumatic events, which may determine individual differences in the tendency to repress.

Q: Outline one explanation of repression. OR How has the concept of repression been used to explain forgetting in LTM?

A: Outline Freud's explanation. See 'Emotional factors in forgetting'.

Q: Describe reconstructive memory.

A: Explain that memory involves the active process of reconstruction. See 'Reconstructive memory' and the APFCC.

Q: Outline two factors that influence reconstructive memory.

A: Culture and schema. See 'Reconstructive memory' and the APFCC.

Q: Outline two factors that influence the accuracy of EWT.

A: Reconstructions and the influence of schema, language, or emotional factors. See 'Reconstructive memory', 'Eyewitness testimony', and the APFCC.

Comparison questions (2 + 2 + 2 marks or 3 + 3 marks)

Example exam question: Give two or three differences between...   (3 + 3 marks or 2 + 2 + 2 marks)

Q: Describe three differences between STM and LTM.

A: Encoding, capacity, and duration, or you could consider differences in forgetting. See 'STM and LTM' and 'Forgetting'.

Criticism questions (3 + 3 marks)

Example exam questions: Give two criticisms of...   (3 + 3 marks)
Outline one explanation and give one criticism...   (3 + 3 marks)

EXAM TIP: Don't just state, elaborate, i.e., explain your criticism fully to gain all of the marks. You need to be able to criticise the explanations/theory and research/APFCC studies. Make sure you clearly relate the criticisms to the theory or research. Use your knowledge of methodological weaknesses, for example:

Ψ   The artificial experimental tasks (learning word lists or nonsense syllables) lack mundane realism, i.e., they bear little resemblance to how we use memory in real life. Consequently, the findings may only be representative of this artificial context and so lack external validity as they have limited generalisability to other settings. It may well be the case that encoding, capacity, or duration are not the same as predicted by the research when the information that is learned is more meaningful.

Ψ   The controlled conditions of the laboratory experiment do enable good control of confounding variables and so we can be confident that the independent variable (IV) has been isolated and is therefore responsible for the changes in the dependent variable (DV). This supports the internal validity of the findings.

Ψ   Participant reactivity when being researched may lead to biased results, i.e., the IV's effect may be due to the reaction of the participants to being observed. Thus, they may overperform as would be predicted by the Hawthorne effect or underperform due to evaluation apprehension. This means that findings may lack internal validity.

OR you may be asked to criticise the above explanations/theories. Again, two are likely to be asked for so make sure you know two in sufficient detail for 3 marks each.

Q: Give two criticisms of the multi-store model OR an alternative to the multi-store model.

A: Consider the positive and negative evaluation in 'Models of memory'. For example: Multi-store: 1) It doesn't account for memory without rehearsal, e.g., flashbulb; 2) There is more than one type of STM and LTM and so they are not single stores. Levels of processing: 1) May confuse effort with depth; 2) Descriptive not explanatory. Working memory model: 1) Lacks understanding of the central executive; 2) Accounts for STM as an active processor.

Q: Give two criticisms of an explanation of forgetting in STM.

A: Trace decay: has it faded away or is it caused by displacement? It is difficult to verify trace decay and so lacks scientific validity, i.e., you can't measure what you don't know!

Q: Give two criticisms of an explanation for forgetting in LTM.

A: Interference: mundane realism, and it is disputed by Tulving and Psotka's study (1971). See 'Forgetting'.

Q: Give two criticisms for the explanations of the role of emotional factors in forgetting.

A: Mundane realism, and high emotional arousal has contradictory effects, as it can improve or inhibit memory, and it is not clear why or which effect will occur. See 'Emotional factors in forgetting'.

Q: Give two criticisms of reconstructive memory.

A: High ecological validity, but may overemphasise the inaccuracy of memory. See 'Reconstructive memory'.

Q: Give two criticisms of eyewitness testimony research.

A: Positive applications, but must question the external validity. See 'Eyewitness testimony'.

Example Essay Question on Eyewitness Testimony

Consider what psychological research (theories and/or studies) has told us about how to improve the reliability of eyewitness testimony. **(18 marks)**

Paragraph 1: AO1

Ψ **Show you understand the question—Define eyewitness testimony and identify research that has suggested ways to improve the reliability of EWT**

Eyewitness testimony (EWT) refers to evidence supplied by people who witness a specific event or crime, relying only on their memory. Statements often include descriptions of the criminal (facial appearance and other identifiable characteristics) and subsequent identification, and details of the crime scene (e.g., the sequence of events, time of day, if others witnessed the event, and so on). As the question suggests, the reliability of EWT may be distorted by the effect of schemas on reconstruction (Bartlett, 1932). It can also be distorted by the use of leading questions and post-event information, which can lead to memory blending (Loftus' research), and the effect of emotional factors in EWT on memory. Therefore it is research into these areas that has yielded insights into ways to improve the reliability of EWT.

Paragraph 2: AO2—Evidence for, i.e., research that shows that EWT has been improved

Ψ **Applications of Loftus' research**

Research on EWT has had a positive impact on police procedures. For example, the cognitive interview has been developed based on Loftus' findings on leading questions and post-event information. Research suggests the cognitive interview yields twice as many correct statements as the standard police interview (Geiselman et al.), and so this has improved the reliability of EWT. The cognitive interview also aims to increase contextual cues (witnesses should be asked to recall the scene in order of the events), minimise distractions, and reduce eyewitness anxiety. Thus, research on cue-dependent memory and emotional factors has also been applied to improve the accuracy of EWT.

Paragraph 3: AO2—Evidence against, i.e., question the improvements

Ψ **Evaluation of the insights**

However, the validity of the above insights into sources of bias can be questioned. Whilst Loftus and Palmer, and Loftus and Zanni have demonstrated the effect of leading questions and post-event information, this research was carried out in the artificial conditions of the laboratory and demand characteristics may have been revealed. Participants may have guessed the experimental hypothesis and acted accordingly. Consequently, the internal and external (ecological) validity of the research must be questioned and caution must be taken in generalising these findings to real-life EWT. Thus, the extent to which psychological research can improve the reliability of EWT is limited because of the methodological weaknesses of the research.

Ψ **Question on inaccuracy of EWT**

The extent to which EWT testimony needs to be improved can also be questioned, as real-life EWT has higher accuracy than the research would suggest. Yuille and Cutshall (1986) have found impressive accuracy in people's recall of the main events of a crime. Furthermore, research suggests that it is easier to distort minor details than key details, which raises further doubt as to what extent improvements need to be made in real-life EWT.

Conclusion: AO2

The research findings have been applied successfully in the cognitive interview and so psychological research has helped improve the reliability of EWT. However, there are methodological issues that limit the generalisability of psychological research to real-life EWT, but the evident applications do overcome these criticisms to some extent.

Human Memory Essay Plans

1. Outline and evaluate the multi-store model of memory. (18 marks)

Paragraph 1 AO1

Define the multi-store model and explain the main features including the three stores and the process of rehearsal.

Paragraph 2 AO2

Research that demonstrates differences in encoding, capacity, and duration between STM and LTM supports the distinction between STM and LTM, as identified by the multi-store model. Further research evidence in support of the multi-store model includes Murdock's (1962) serial position curve, and Glanzer and Cunitz's (1966) research using an interference task, which supported the importance of rehearsal. The brain damage case studies also support a distinction between STM and LTM, as KF suffered damage to his STM but not his LTM (Warrington & Shallice, 1972). Remember to use link sentences to keep this evaluative and not descriptive. Restrict yourself to the findings and conclusions and use these as evidence. So do not describe in detail, make sure you summarise.

Paragraph 3 AO2

The brain damage case studies also provide evidence against the multi-store model, which claims that memory is divided into single stores, in several ways. KF's STM was clearly more complex than a single store because his visual memory was better than his auditory memory. Research has shown that LTM is also not a single store, as both declarative and procedural knowledge have been identified. This indicates that the multi-store model is over simplistic. There is also the case of HM, which demonstrated that rehearsal may be an oversimplification as he was able to form new STM and hold it there, i.e., rehearsal, but was not able to transfer this information to LTM. Hence, this case study suggests the transfer mechanism may be more complex than simply rehearsal. Rehearsal is not always necessary for memories to become permanent, as in flashbulb memory, which challenges the multi-store emphasis on this. The levels of processing theory also contradicts the multi-store model as it suggests that rehearsal is not important, rather it is the depth of processing that creates memories. The multi-store model is also criticised because it portrays STM and LTM as passive stores when they are active processors. The working memory model demonstrated this is true of STM and so it expanded on the multi-store model to improve on its reductionism (oversimplification). It does however support the STM/LTM distinction identified by the multi-store model. A further criticism is that transfer of information is presented as a one-way process whereas the interference explanation of forgetting shows that information flow is two-way.

Conclusion AO2

Weigh up the strengths and weaknesses. Bear in mind that whilst there may appear to be more weaknesses, the multi-store model was responsible for inspiring further research that improved and expanded on its original ideas. Also, as you must be aware, STM/LTM is a useful distinction when considering memory.

2. Outline and evaluate an alternative to the multi-store model of memory. (18 marks)

Paragraph 1 AO1

Define levels of processing and outline the main features of this model including the three levels of processing and how this explains why rehearsal is not always necessary.

Paragraph 2 AO2

Research evidence in support of the levels of processing theory is Craik and Tulving (1975), Hyde and Jenkins (1973), and Bransford (1979). Also in support is research that has expanded upon the original forms of processing, e.g., elaboration, organisation, and distinctiveness. Other positive criticisms include the fact that it recognises memory as an active process and has practical applications. You could evaluate the model as having real-life validity, e.g., distinctiveness explains why we learn some things quickly, and flashbulb memory.

Paragraph 3 AO2

To challenge the model, include criticisms of the research such as the weaknesses of laboratory experiments, e.g., reductionism, mundane realism, and external validity. Also, the theory is circular and descriptive rather than explanatory. Deep processing is not always best as it depends on the nature of the material and might be confusing effort with depth. Also use the other models to evaluate this one. It fails to consider the structure of memory, i.e., it doesn't consider the memory stores suggested by the multi-store model and supported by the working memory model.

Conclusion AO2

Weigh up the strengths and weaknesses.

OR

Paragraph 1 AO1

Define working memory and outline the main features of this model including the central executive, which controls the slave systems: the articulatory-phonological loop and the visuo-spatial sketchpad.

Paragraph 2 AO2

Research that supports the model is based on the dual-task technique, e.g., Hitch and Baddeley (1976) and Baddeley and Lewis (1981). Positive criticisms include the fact that it recognises STM as an active processor and that it is not a single passive unit. Also the central executive links memory to attention. The practical applications of the model are that it explains verbal reasoning, mental arithmetic, reading, and planning.

Paragraph 3 AO2

Negative criticisms include the fact that not a great deal is known about the central executive, as it is difficult to verify an abstract concept. It is probably an oversimplification to see the central executive as one system. Only the articulatory-phonological loop has been explored in any detail and so research is lacking on the visuo-spatial sketchpad.

Conclusion AO2

Weigh up the strengths and weaknesses.

3. Outline and evaluate two explanations of forgetting. (18 marks)

Paragraph 1 AO1/AO2

Define forgetting. Outline and evaluate one explanation, e.g., interference. Make sure you distinguish between proactive (forwards, old to new) and retroactive (backwards, new to old). Evaluation includes the fact that it has little mundane realism and therefore lacks generalisability to real life. It is really a product of the artificial tasks conducted in the laboratory as it is rare in real life that two responses are attached to the same stimulus, which is when interference can occur. The study by Tulving and Psotka (1971) provides an excellent criticism. It showed that when asked to recall a word list, different items are recalled each time. This suggests forgetting occurs due to a lack of accessibility rather than interference, which causes a lack of availability, meaning the same items should be recalled each time. Also when given cues, the effect of retroactive interference disappeared. Thus, cue-dependent forgetting is perhaps a better alternative to interference theory.

Paragraph 2 AO1/AO2

Outline cue-dependent forgetting including the encoding specificity principle, state-dependent memory, and context-dependent memory. Evaluate this explanation as being successful in accounting for the fact that different items were recalled each time in Tulving and Psotka's study as it shows that forgetting is due to retrieval failure, and so a lack of accessibility rather than availability. Also discuss the positive applications of the model, e.g., mnemonics and advertising.

Paragraph 3/conclusion AO2

Weigh up the two explanations, concluding that cue-dependent forgetting probably offers more insights and has more real-world validity than interference theory, but it does depend on whether the memory failure is due to availability or accessibility.

4. Consider the strengths and weaknesses of explanations of forgetting. (18 marks)

(The plan has drawn from explanations of forgetting in LTM. Note, the question may specify STM or LTM. Interference and cue-dependent are the explanations covered in the plan but you could write about repression and reconstructive memory if you prefer.)

5. Outline and evaluate psychological research (theories and/or studies) into flashbulb memory. (18 marks)

Paragraph 1 AO1

Define flashbulb memory, and outline the characteristics identified by Brown and Kulik (1977) and illustrate with examples.

Paragraph 2 AO2

Evidence that flashbulb memories may be inaccurate and subject to the same forgetting as any other memories includes McCloskey et al.'s research (1988).

Paragraph 3 AO2

However, Conway et al. (1994) criticised McCloskey et al.'s research and claimed the reason that the flashbulb memories were not accurate was because their test event did not have important consequences in the participants' lives and this is why it wasn't remembered. Conway et al.'s research demonstrates much higher accuracy. Also Cahill and McGaugh (1988) have proposed that flashbulb memories are a biological mechanism and this may be an evolved adaptive response. This further supports the argument that they are accurate, as an inaccurate form of memory would not have evolved from natural selection.

Conclusion AO2

Weigh up the extent of accuracy.

6. Outline and evaluate psychological research (theories and/or studies) into the role of repression in forgetting. (18 marks)

Paragraph 1 AO1

Define repression and outline the main features of this explanation including the terms emotionally threatening content, anxiety, defence mechanism, repression into the unconscious, and illustrate with examples, e.g., forgetting homework or a dental appointment.

Paragraph 2 AO2

Evidence to support the explanation was Freud's own research 'With a white sheet', and Levinger and Clark's (1961) experiment.

Paragraph 3 AO2

Evidence against includes criticisms of the research. For example, Freud used case studies and so generalisability is an issue. The abstract concepts are difficult to operationalise, so verification or falsification is difficult to establish, meaning his research lacks scientific validity. Levinger and Clark have tried to give repression scientific validity with their experiment. This was not completely successful in that although if tested immediately their results did support repression, when recall was tested later, as Parkin (1993) did in his replication, the emotionally charged words were actually recalled better, which contradicts repression as an explanation. Also, this artificial research lacks mundane realism and so may not represent repression in the real world and therefore may lack external validity. It may be less representative of society today, which is much more permissive than the Victorian society of Freud's day. Thus, the explanation is a product of the context of the time and this constrains its generalisability to the current context and so it may be era-dependent and context-bound.

Conclusion AO2

The validity of the research to support repression can be seriously criticised. This reduces the meaningfulness of the findings and means that repression may lack truth as an explanation. However, there are many real-life accounts to support it, for example criminals who rarely recall their crime (how convenient!), and victims of child abuse. Thus, it may well be that a satisfactory way of testing for repression has not yet been identified but that it does work and so has validity as an explanation.

7. Consider what psychological research (theories and/or studies) has told us about the role of emotional factors in forgetting. (18 marks)

See 'Essay plans for questions 4 and 5'.

8. Outline and evaluate the insights provided by psychological research (theories and/or studies) into reconstructive memory. (18 marks)

Paragraph 1 AO1

Define reconstructive memory and outline Bartlett's (1932) research 'The War of the Ghosts' and schema theory.

Paragraph 2 AO2

Evaluate the implications of his research, i.e., how it explains the fallibility of memory. Also how it accounts for the influence of prejudice and stereotypes. Schemas have been implicated in the initial storage and retrieval of information. It shows that memory is ethnocentric and what distortion to be aware of in memories. It explains people's mental blocks, i.e., when you get someone's name completely wrong because in your schema they look like a Kevin or a Sharon. And of course applications to eyewitness testimony.

Paragraph 3 AO2

Bartlett's work has strengths and weaknesses. It is qualitative research as he was looking for meanings and is more representative than most research of real-life memory. But taking the qualitative approach does mean scientific validity is reduced. His research lacked rigour as participants were asked to recall at different times with no control or standardisation implemented. Thus, confounding variables may also be responsible for the forgetting, and researcher-bias and participant reactivity may have occurred. Consequently, internal validity may be limited. This reduces the meaningfulness of the findings and so value of the research, but on the other hand it does have real-world validity.

Conclusion AO2

Weigh up the strengths and limitations.

9. Outline and evaluate the insights provided by psychological research (theories and/or studies) into eyewitness testimony (EWT). (18 marks)

See 'Example essay question on eyewitness testimony'.

10. Consider what psychological research(theories and/or studies) has told us about how to improve the accuracy of eyewitness testimony (EWT). (18 marks)

See 'Example essay question on eyewitness testimony'.

Human Memory Crib Sheets

Cross-reference with Brody and Dwyer's revision guide, the human memory APFCCs, findings/conclusions (in the Appendices), essay plans, and AO1 revision summary.

Definitions

Memory: ....

....

Short-term memory: ....

....

Long-term memory: ....

....

Multi-store model: ....

....

Forgetting: ....

....

Flashbulb memory: ....

....

Repression: ....

....

Eyewitness testimony: ....

....

Reconstructive memory: ....

....

Leading questions: ....

....

Differences between STM and LTM

Encoding: ....

....

Capacity: ....

....

Duration: ....

Models of memory

Multi-store model (Atkinson & Shiffrin, 1968): ....
....

AO2: ....
....

Levels of processing (Craik & Lockhart, 1972): ....
....

AO2: ....
....

Working memory model (Baddeley & Hitch, 1974): ....
....

AO2: ....

....

Forgetting in LTM

Trace decay: ....
....

AO2: ....

Interference theory: ....
....

AO2: ....

Cue-dependent forgetting/retrieval failure: ....
....

The encoding specificity principle: ....
....

Context- and state-dependent memory: ....
....

AO2: ....

Forgetting in STM

Trace decay: ....
....

AO2: ....

Displacement: ....
....

AO2: ....

Emotional factors in forgetting

Flashbulb memory: ....
.... 43

Biological mechanism: ....
....

AO2 accuracy: ....
....

Repression: ....
....

Research evidence: ....
....

AO2 validity in today's permissive society: ....
....

Reconstructive memory (Bartlett, 1932)

The War of the Ghosts: ....
....

Distortions to the original story: ....
....

Schema (knowledge of the world) theory: ....
....

Eyewitness testimony (EWT)

Leading questions: ....
....

Post-event information: ....
....

Memory blending: ....
....

AO2 accuracy: ....
....

Real-life EWT: ....
....

Attachments in Development Learning Objectives

On completion of this topic you should be familiar with the following.

The development and variety of attachments

- Define attachment and describe and evaluate the development of attachments, e.g., the stages in the development of attachment suggested by Schaffer and Emerson (1964).
- Critically consider individual variation in attachments through Ainsworth and Bell's Strange Situation research and the three types of attachment identified by this, and be able to define secure and insecure attachment.
- Assess the contribution of the infant (temperament hypothesis) and the caregiver (sensitivity hypothesis) to attachment type.
- Define cross-cultural variations in attachments and be able to describe and evaluate these.
- Describe the Aims, Procedures, Findings, Conclusions, and Criticisms (APFCC) for a study of individual differences in attachment, e.g., Ainsworth and Bell's (1970) 'Strange Situation', and a study of cross-cultural variation in attachments, e.g., Van IJzendoorn and Kroonenberg's (1988) 'meta-analysis of Strange Situation studies'.
- Describe and evaluate the explanations of attachment: psychodynamic, learning theory, social learning theory, and Bowlby's theory.

Deprivation and privation

- Define deprivation and privation.
- Describe and evaluate Bowlby's (1953) maternal deprivation hypothesis including the evidence on which it is based.
- Consider the effects of privation and give the APFCC for a study of the long-term effects of privation, e.g., Hodges and Tizard's (1989) 'study of institutionalised children'.
- Distinguish between separation, deprivation, and privation.
- Assess the reversibility/irreversibility of deprivation and privation.

Critical issue—Day care

- Define day care, cognitive development, and social development.
- Assess the positive and negative effects of day care on infant attachment and consequent cognitive and social development.
- Consider the issue of variation in the quality of day care.

Cross-reference the above learning objectives with the Specification and fill in the self-assessment box below on completion of the topic.

SELF-ASSESSMENT BOX

☺ **Which of the above do you know?**

☹ **Are there any gaps in your knowledge that need to be targeted during revision?**

Attachments in Development

For details, see Eysenck's textbook (page 89) and Brody and Dwyer's revision guide (page 39). Fill in the gaps using the letter clues provided and use the cues in the table to guide your note taking.

Ask yourself: 'What makes my life meaningful?' The two most common answers are f_____ and r_____ partners. Bowlby (1969) suggests that early a_____ are a basis for all future relationships, as an i_____ w_____ m_____ about relationships is formed. Whilst this should not be accepted without question, it does demonstrate the significance of our e____ attachments.

Definition of attachment

Maccoby's (1980) key characteristics of attachment
Ψ Seeking proximity to primary caregiver.
Ψ Distress on separation (separation anxiety).
Ψ Pleasure when reunited.
Ψ General orientation of behaviour towards primary caregiver.

Why do infants form attachments?	
Short-term benefits	**Long-term benefits**

Using this in the exam

AO1 question:

Explain what is meant by the terms secure and insecure attachment .   (3 + 3 marks)

Essay question:

This content could be used as AO1 (the characteristics and benefits of attachment) and AO2 in an essay question as evidence that some of the characteristics of attachment may be universal, and so less subject to variation.

To what extent is there variation in the development of attachments?   (18 marks)

Stages in the Development of Attachment

For details, see Eysenck's textbook (page 91) and Brody and Dwyer's revision guide (page 44). Fill in the gaps using the letter clues provided and use the cues in the table to guide your note taking.

It is widely held that a_____ develops through a series of s_____. Four stages predict a pattern of d_____ in the first 18 months of the child's life. The research by S_____ and E_____ (1964) provides the most widely used account of the stage development of attachment. They researched 60 infants using the n_____ o_____ research method and measured attachment based on two key behaviours that indicate attachment: 1) s_____ p_____, and 2) s_____ a_____. Bowlby (1969) and Ainsworth et al. (1978) suggest similar phases in development thus supporting the reliability and validity of the stage accounts of the development of attachment.

Stages in the development of attachment (Schaffer & Emerson, 1964)		
Stage	**Age**	**Characteristics**
Asocial		
Indiscriminate attachments		
Specific attachments (and subsequently multiple attachments)		

Evaluation of Schaffer and Emerson's stage theory	
Evidence for	**Evidence against**
Ψ The stages appear to be correct.	Ψ Infant sociability—there is research evidence that babies may not be asocial.
Ψ Infants do display separation protest and stranger anxiety.	Ψ The skin-to-skin hypothesis (Klaus & Kennell, 1976)

Using this in the exam

AO1 question:
Explain the development of attachments. (6 marks)

Essay question:
To what extent are there variations in the development of attachments? (18 marks)
The content on this page could be used as evidence against variation as it shows that the pattern of development is fairly universal.

Individual Differences in Attachment

For details, see Eysenck's textbook (page 93) and Brody and Dwyer's revision guide (page 46). Fill in the gaps using the letter clues provided and use the cues in the table to guide your note taking.

The S_____ S_____ is a controlled observation study designed by A_____ and B___ (1970) as measure of a_____. By placing infants in conditions of high and low stress in an unfamiliar environment—the Strange Situation—they tested the q_____ of the infant's attachment to its c_____ whilst the infant was aged between ___ and ___ months.

You could also be asked an APFCC question on this so please complete the Ainsworth and Bell (1970) APFCC.

The Strange Situation (Ainsworth & Bell, 1970)
Ψ What key behaviours are measured in the Strange Situation as indicators of attachment?   • ....   • ....   • ....
Definition of secure attachment
Definition of insecure attachment
Secure attachment type
Secure (70%) Type B
Insecure attachment types
Avoidant (20%) Type A
Resistant (10%) Type C
Disorganised Type D   Ψ This attachment type was suggested by Main and Soloman (1986) as a criticism of the attachment types identified by Ainsworth and Bell.

Evaluation of the Strange Situation

Reliability = consistency

Ψ How is reliability tested?

Ψ Research evidence (Main, Kaplan, & Cassidy, 1985).

Validity = truth

Ψ Criterion validity.

Ψ Research evidence (Sroufe, 1983).

Ψ The research demonstrates a correlation not causation between attachment and later social development. Why?

Attachment type or relationship between infant and caregiver?

Ψ Research evidence that attachment is a stable individual difference (Sroufe, 1983).

Ψ Research evidence that attachment is not a stable individual difference but depends on the relationship between the child and the caregiver (Main & Weston, 1981).

Alternative explanations for individual differences

The temperament hypothesis (Kagan, 1984)	The sensitivity hypothesis (Ainsworth, 1982)	Transactional model An interaction of the infant's innate temperament and the sensitivity of the caregiver.

Using this in the exam

AO1 questions:

What is meant by the terms secure and insecure attachment? (3 + 3 marks)

Describe the APFCC of one study in which individual differences in attachment have been investigated. (6 marks)

Describe the findings (or conclusions) of research into individual differences in attachment. (6 marks)

Outline two factors that influence attachment type. (3 + 3 marks)
For example, infant's temperament and maternal sensitivity.

Outline two individual differences in attachments. (3 + 3 marks)
For example, the attachment types identified by Ainsworth and the infant's innate temperament as identified by Kagan.

Describe the Strange Situation method and detail how it has been employed across research studies. (6 marks)

Essay question:

Outline and evaluate psychological research (theories and/or studies) into individual differences in attachment. (18 marks)
Evidence for individual differences can be based on the material on this page, and evidence against (that attachment is universal) can be based on 'Attachments in development' and 'Stages in the development of attachment'.

Cross-cultural Variations in Attachment Types

For details, see Eysenck's textbook (page 99) and Brody and Dwyer's revision guide (page 47). Fill in the gaps using the letter clues provided and use the cues in the table to guide your note taking.

The S_____ S_____ has been used to investigate attachment t_____ in countries other than A_____, where Ainsworth developed the method. If attachment is in____ then the attachment types should be fairly u_____.

You could also be asked an APFCC question on this so please complete the APFCC on cross-cultural variations.

Definition of cross-cultural variations

Cross-cultural variations in attachment (Van IJzendoorn & Kroonenberg, 1988)			
Country	Type of attachment		Differences in childrearing practices
	Secure	Avoidant	Resistant	

Country	Secure	Avoidant	Resistant	Differences in childrearing practices
USA	65%	21%	14%	Mothers spend a great deal of time in close contact with the child.
WEST GERMANY	57%	35%	8%	Contact with mother but greater interpersonal distance between parents and child is the cultural norm.
ISRAEL	64%	7%	29%	Children raised communally as part of kibbutz culture.
JAPAN	68%	5%	27%	Children very rarely separated from mother, so the Strange Situation is extremely stressful.

Description	Evaluation
Ψ Do the findings show any consistency? Ψ What variation exists between individualistic and collectivist cultures?	Ψ Consistency suggests universality in attachments. Ψ Variation within cultures is greater than variation between cultures. Ψ Measurement of cross-cultural attachment is invalid as it uses a technique developed in one culture to study another culture—the Strange Situation is an imposed etic.

Using this in the exam

AO1 questions:

Explain what is meant by the terms attachment and cross-cultural variations in attachment.	(3 + 3 marks)
Describe the APFCC of one study in which cross-cultural variations in attachment have been investigated.	(6 marks)
Describe the findings (or conclusions) of research into cross-cultural variations in attachment.	(6 marks)
Outline two factors that influence cross-cultural variations in attachment.	(3 + 3 marks)
Outline two cross-cultural variations in attachment.	(3 + 3 marks)

Essay question:

Outline and evaluate psychological research (theories and/or studies) into cross-cultural variations in attachment.   (18 marks)
Use the content in this section as evidence for and against cross-cultural variation. You could also use content from 'Attachments in development' and 'Stages in the development of attachment' as evidence of universality.

Explanations of Attachment

For details, see Eysenck's textbook (page 103) and Brody and Dwyer's revision guide (page 48). Use the cues in the table to guide your note taking and fill in the gaps using the letter clues provided.

Psychodynamic theory
The explanation is based on F_____'s theory of psychosexual d_____. Infants are in the o____ stage when forming attachments and so the focus is on o____ s_____. The emphasis is on the i_____ psyche as an explanation of attachment.
Ψ 'Cupboard-love': libidinal desires are satisfied. Ψ Prototype for future relationships. **Evaluation** Ψ Harlow's (1959) research contradicts 'cupboard-love'. Ψ Schaffer and Emerson's (1964) research suggests that approximately 40% of infants do not attach to the primary caregiver.

Learning theories
According to learning theories, attachment like all b_____ is s_____ by the en_____. Based on the behavioural explanations of c_____ conditioning and o_____ conditioning, attachment is a consequence of ass_____ and r_____. The emphasis is on the e_____, i.e., the external, as the explanation for attachment.
Ψ Classical conditioning—associating the mother with food. Ψ Operant conditioning—the mother is a source of positive reinforcement (e.g., drive-reduction). **Evaluation** Ψ Also contradicted by Harlow's (1959) research due to emphasis on 'cupboard love'. Ψ Learning theory is reductionist.

Social learning theories

This explanation is that attachment is learned through o_____ and i_____ of role models (e.g., the parents) and re_____. This requires some intervening m_____ p_____, which is not taken into account by traditional learning theories as they ignore the role of co_____.

Ψ Learn by observation and imitation.

Ψ Parents teach their children to love them and social skills through:
  • Modelling.

  • Direct instruction.

  • Social facilitation.

Evaluation
Ψ Has increased understanding of the role of interactional processes.

Ψ Does not account for the emotional intensity of attachments.

Bowlby's theory

E_____ and p_____ theory influenced Bowlby's (1951) work. Thus, he supports ethology's claim that attachment is i_____ and must be formed within a c_____ p_____ (7 months–3 years), and that its main purpose is to promote s_____. As with psychodynamic theory, Bowlby suggested that attachment acts as a t_____ for all future relationships. He expanded on this with the concept of m_____, which means that attachments form a h_____ where the infant has one main attachment, and this is a special bond different from all other attachments.

Attachment is an adaptive process

Ψ Safety and survival—which theory is this based upon?

Ψ Innate: programmed to attach, and being a biological mechanism, it has a critical period (ends between 1 and 3 years). There is evidence that it is innate—what do babies imprint onto?

Ψ Internal working model—which theory is this based upon?

Ψ Monotropy: one special relationship.

Ψ Attachment is a psychological 'stay-close' mechanism where the mother is used as a secure base.

Ψ Attachment is reciprocal (two-way)—what role do 'social releasers' play?

Evaluation

Ψ Positive applications and influence on further research.

Ψ Internal working model is deterministic and may not be a template for future relationships. Group Socialisation Theory (GST) emphasises the importance of peer relationships.

Ψ Schaffer and Emerson (1964) provide evidence that multiple attachments may be equally strong, so attachments are not necessarily hierarchical, which suggests that attachment may not be monotropic.

Ψ Evolutionary theory is post hoc.

Using this in the exam

AO1 questions:

Outline and evaluate one or more psychological explanations of attachment.   (3 + 3 marks)
Outline one explanation of attachment.   (6 marks)

Essay questions:

Outline and evaluate explanations of attachment.   (18 marks)
Outline and evaluate two explanations of attachment.   (18 marks)
Consider the extent to which psychological theories have been successful in
explaining attachment.   (18 marks)

Deprivation and Privation

For details, see Eysenck's textbook (page 116) and Brody and Dwyer's revision guide (page 51). Use the cues in the table to guide your note taking and fill in the gaps using the letter clues provided. You could also be asked an APFCC question on the effects of deprivation or the effects of privation, so please complete the APFCCs.

Definitions	
Deprivation (loss of)	**Privation** (lack of)

Short-term effects of deprivation

Robertson and Bowlby's (1952) PDD model
- Protest.

- Despair.

- Detachment.

Evaluation
Ψ Oversimplistic, as it does not account for individual differences.

Ψ Bond disruption may not occur.

Long-term effects of deprivation

The maternal deprivation hypothesis
- Affectionless psychopathy.

> **EXAM TIP**: Bowlby uses the term 'maternal' to refer to the significant caregiver who is not necessarily the mother.

Evaluation
Ψ Positive impact on hospital and institutional practices.

Ψ The concept of deprivation (Rutter, 1972).

Ψ Rutter criticised Bowlby for confusing causation with correlation. Maladjustment may be caused by other factors.

Ψ It is a product of the context—it suited the political agenda at the time.

Institutionalisation and anaclitic depression

Bowlby's research is based on studies by:

Ψ Spitz and Wolf (1946).

Ψ Goldfarb (1947).

Evaluation

Ψ Deprived of stimulation and attention, not just maternal care.

Ψ Widdowson (1951) supports the importance of emotional care.

Hospitalisation

Ψ Douglas (1975).

Ψ Quinton and Rutter (1976).

Evaluation

Ψ Clarke and Clarke (1976) suggest home problems may be a third factor in the correlation between separation and social and cognitive development.

Ψ Bowlby et al. (1956) found bond disruption can be minimised.

Distinguishing separation, deprivation, and privation

Robertson and Robertson (1971) distinguished separation (no bond disruption) from deprivation (bond disruption). Rutter (1972) has criticised Bowlby's concept of deprivation as too general as it is used to account for d_____ types of early experience, which have quite different e_____. He distinguishes between d_____ and p_____. Rather than rejecting it, Rutter has redefined Bowlby's hypothesis. His research on adolescents living on the Isle of Wight led him to conclude that separation does not inevitably result in m_____ and delinquency. He found that family discord due to d_____ was four times more likely to lead to maladjustment than separation as a result of physical i_____ or d_____ of the mother. Thus, the reason for the separation, i.e., family discord, is more influential than the separation itself. This expands on the maternal deprivation hypothesis as o_____ f_____ involved in maladjustment have been identified. The family d_____ may have prevented b_____ from forming and so the adolescents experienced p_____, which is more likely to lead to d_____y than d_____.

Case studies of privation	
Czech twins (Koluchová, 1976, 1991)	**Evaluation** Ψ Adverse effects can be reversed.
Genie (Curtiss, 1989)	Ψ Methodological criticisms.
Children of the Holocaust (Freud & Dann, 1951)	

Irreversibility vs. reversibility

Hodges and Tizard's (1989) study of institutionalised children

Bowlby claimed the negative effects of deprivation could not be undone. Affectionless psychopathy was a permanent retardation of emotional development. This is deterministic as it suggests we have no control over our own behaviour.

Ψ Tizard et al.'s research reveals that the effects can be reversible and so can be used as a criticism of Bowlby.

Ψ The children's difficulties in relationships outside the foster home do support Bowlby's concept of an internal working model.

Ψ Harris' (1997) Group Socialisation Theory (GST) contradicts the internal working model.

Conclusions

Development is more flexible and less deterministic than the maternal d_____ h_____ suggests. As the research evidence is c_____ we must avoid drawing cause-and-effect conclusions. Other factors such as in_____ and si_____ differences contribute to the effects and this leads to multiple outcomes. Thus, m_____ is a possible but not inevitable consequence of maternal deprivation.

Using this in the exam

AO1 questions:

Explain what is meant by the terms deprivation and privation.	(3 + 3 marks)
Outline the effects of deprivation.	(6 marks)
Outline the effects of privation.	(6 marks)
Outline Bowlby's maternal deprivation hypothesis.	(6 marks)
Give two criticisms of Bowlby's maternal deprivation hypothesis.	(3 + 3 marks)
Outline the APFCC of a study into the effects of privation.	(6 marks)
Outline two factors that influence deprivation and/or privation.	(3 + 3 marks)

Essay questions:

Consider what research (theories and/or studies) into deprivation/privation has told us about the reversibility/irreversibility of deprivation/privation. (18 marks)

Consider the extent to which Bowlby has contributed to our understanding of attachments. (18 marks)
Use his theory and the maternal deprivation hypothesis.

Consider whether research studies support the view that maternal deprivation/privation can have long-term effects. (18 marks)

Compare and contrast the effects of deprivation and privation. (18 marks)

Consider the extent to which research supports Bowlby's maternal deprivation hypothesis. (18 marks)

Outline and evaluate psychological research (theories and/or studies) into deprivation/privation and consider how this research helps us to understand the effects of deprivation/privation. (18 marks)

Day Care

For details, see Eysenck's textbook (page 128) and Brody and Dwyer's revision guide (page 58). Fill in the gaps using the letter clues provided and use the cues in the table to guide your note taking.

This is a practical app_____ of psychological research on attachments because it raises the controversial issue of whether day care has negative effects on children's c_____ and s_____ development. There are arguments for and against d__ c___. The argument against is that any s_____ from the c_____ is harmful according to some interpretations of the m_____ d_____ hypothesis. The argument for is that day care benefits some children. For example, pre-school programmes such as O_____ Headstart were set up as a way of compensating for so___ disadvantage.

Definition of day care

Types of day care

Day nurseries

Ψ Kagan et al.'s (1980) study that showed no difference between nursery and home care.

Ψ Andersson's (1992) longitudinal study in Sweden.

Ψ Operation Headstart.

Childminders

Ψ Mayall and Petrie (1983).

Ψ Bryant et al. (1980).

Definition of social development

Effects on social development

Positive effects

Ψ Sociability (Shea, 1981).

Ψ Advanced peer relations (Clarke-Stewart et al., 1994).

Ψ Day care may not affect the security of the child/caregiver attachment (Clarke-Stewart et al., 1994, and Roggman et al., 1994).

Negative effects

Ψ Some find it a threatening experience (Pennebaker et al., 1981).

Ψ Day care can have negative effects on the relationship between infant and caregiver:

• Increased risk of insecure attachments (Belsky & Rovine, 1988).

• It may damage the infant/caregiver relationship if it occurs before the age of 2 years (Sroufe, 1990).

Definition of cognitive development

Effects on cognitive development

Positive effects

Ψ Higher IQ on school entry (Burchinal et al., 1989).

Ψ Verbal and mathematical ability tests (Broberg et al., 1997).

Ψ School performance is highest in those who enter day care before 1 year of age (Andersson et al., 1992).

Negative effects

Ψ Conversational differences (Tizard, 1979).

Ψ Effects of being in day care for 6 hours + per day (Clarke-Stewart et al., 1994).

Individual differences

Ψ Effects depend on attachment type (Egeland & Hiester, 1995).

Ψ Effects determined by an interaction of quality of day care and maternal sensitivity.

Ψ The level of stimulation in the home environment.

Improving Day Care

For details, see Eysenck's textbook (page 132) and Brody and Dwyer's revision guide (page 61). Use the cues in the table to guide your note taking and fill in the gaps using the letter clues provided.

With so much governmental pressure on parents to return to work in addition to the economic pressure they face, it may be a mistake to see day care as a choice. Thus, it is important to establish what the effects of day care are and how we can ensure that they are positive. It appears that separation is not the key issue in respect to day care given that some children appear to benefit from day care. Thus, quality of care is the more relevant issue. How would you set about raising and maintaining high quality day care? Which type of day care would you recommend to concerned parents and why?

Consistency of care	Quality of care
Ψ Lack of consistency (Tizard, 1979).	Ψ The amount of verbal interaction between caregiver and child.
Ψ High consistency (Kagan et al., 1980).	Ψ Stimulation.
	Ψ Sensitive emotional care.
Ψ The NICHD study (1997).	Ψ Howes et al.'s (1998) caregiver intervention programme.

Conclusions

Effects vary depending on the q_____ of care, the t____ of day care, the individual differences of the child and the caregiver, and the amount of st_____ in the h____ environment. Hence, effects are subject to great v_____. As the evidence is c_____, cause and effect cannot be inferred as there are many factors involved in the association. Q_____ is perhaps the greatest determinant of whether e_____ are p_____ or n_____. What conclusions can you draw about the effects of day care?

Using this in the exam

AO1 questions:

Explain what is meant by the terms day care, social development, and cognitive development.	(2 + 2 + 2 marks)
Describe two effects of day care.	(3 + 3 marks)
Outline the effects of day care on <u>cognitive/social</u> development.	(6 marks)
Give two effects of day care on <u>cognitive/social</u> development.	(3 + 3 marks)
Outline two factors that influence the effects of day care on <u>social/cognitive</u> development.	(3 + 3 marks)

For example, quality of care and attachment type.

Essay question:

Assess the extent to which psychological research (theories and/or studies) support the view that day care can have a <u>positive/negative</u> effect on <u>social/cognitive</u> development? (18 marks)

EXAM TIP: Underlined parts mean it could be either of the two words.

Attachments in Development APFCCs

A study of individual differences in types of attachment— Ainsworth and Bell's (1970) Strange Situation study

Aims:

Procedures:

Findings:

Conclusions:

Criticisms:

A study of cross-cultural variations in attachment—van IJzendoorn and Kroonenberg's (1988) meta-analysis of Strange Situation studies

Aims:

Procedures:

Findings:

Conclusions:

Criticisms:

A study of the long-term effects of privation—
Hodges and Tizard's (1989) study of institutionalised children

Aims:

Procedures:

Findings:

Conclusions:

Criticisms:

Attachments in Development Revision AO1

Use this as a checklist, i.e., tick off when you feel confident you can answer the following questions and/or have prepared a model answer for each type of question. The range of potential exam questions is finite so you can prepare for all possibilities.

Definition questions (2 + 2 + 2 marks or 3 + 3 marks)

You may be asked to define any of the terms that appear on the Specification, except for those that are given as examples. So cross-reference with the Specification.

> **EXAM TIP**: If you have not included enough content to access all of the marks, give an example.
>
> | | | |
> |---|---|---|
> | Attachment | Secure attachment | Insecure attachment |
> | Cross-cultural variations in attachment | Privation | Day care |
> | Cognitive development | Social development | |

Definitions

Cross-reference with the glossary in the Brody and Dwyer revision guide (pages 193–202).

Example exam question: What is meant by the terms... *[and two or three of the following would be stated]*

Attachment:

Secure attachment:

Insecure attachment:

Cross-cultural variations in attachment:

Privation:
Day care:
Cognitive development:
Social development:

Research questions (6 marks or 3 + 3 marks)

Cross-reference with the completed APFCCs in the appendix of the Brody and Dwyer revision guide (pages 182–185).

Example exam questions: Describe the aims/procedures/findings/conclusions/one criticism
of a study into... *[any two aspects could be specified]* (6 marks)
Describe the findings of research into... (6 marks)
Describe the conclusions of research into... (6 marks)
Give two criticisms of research into... (3 + 3 marks)

EXAM TIP: Allocate your time in the exam as roughly 1 minute per mark, so you have 6 minutes to answer each of the APFCC questions.

Make sure you can give the APFCCs for the following attachments studies:

Q: Outline the APFCC of one study into individual differences in attachments. OR findings/conclusions.

A: Ainsworth and Bell's (1970) Strange Situation, Ainsworth et al. (1978), Ainsworth (1982), and Main and Solomon (1986) if findings/conclusions.

Q: Outline the APFCC of one study into cross-cultural variation in attachments. OR findings/conclusions.

A: Van IJzendoorn and Kroonenberg's (1988) meta-analysis of attachment types across cultures, Sagi et al. (1991), and Grossmann et al. (1985) if findings/conclusions.

Q: Outline the procedures of research that has investigated variations in attachments.

A: Ainsworth and Bell (1970), Ainsworth et al. (1978), Van IJzendoorn and Kroonenberg (1988).

Q: Outline the APFCC of one study into the effects of privation. OR findings/conclusions.

A: Hodges and Tizard's (1989) study of institutionalised children, Rutter (1981), Curtiss (1989), and Freud and Dann (1951) if findings/conclusions.

Explanations/theories questions (6 marks or 3 + 3 marks)

These questions could be worded in a number of ways.

Example exam questions: Describe one explanation of...	(6 marks)
Outline two explanations of...	(3 + 3 marks)
Outline one explanation and give one criticism of...	(3 + 3 marks)
Outline the main features of...	(6 marks)
Outline two factors that explain...	(3 + 3 marks)
Outline two factors that influence...	(3 + 3 marks)
Outline two ways that...	(3 + 3 marks)
Outline two effects of...	(3 + 3 marks)

> **EXAM TIP**: As you will see, the content here overlaps with the APFCCs and relevant research can be included in these questions even though it hasn't been specifically asked for.

Q: Outline the development of attachments.

A: Schaffer and Emerson's (1964) stage account of the development of attachments. See 'Stages in the development of attachment'.

Q: Outline two factors that are important in the development of attachments. OR Outline two factors that influence secure/insecure attachment. OR Outline two factors that influence individual differences in attachments.

A: The infant (temperament hypothesis) and the caregiver (sensitivity hypothesis). See 'Individual differences in attachment'.

Q: Outline two individual differences in attachment.

A: The different attachment types identified by the Strange Situation and the infant's temperament (temperament hypothesis), i.e., innate sociability. See 'Individual differences in attachment', and the APFCCs.

Q: Outline two effects of secure/insecure attachments.

A: Emotional, social (i.e., internal working model), and cognitive effects could be cited. See the characteristics of the three main attachment types in 'Individual differences in attachment'.

Q: Outline two cross-cultural variations in attachments.

A: The differences in attachment types across cultures as summarised by van IJzendoorn and Kroonenberg (1988), e.g., the higher number of avoidant infants in individualistic cultures and the higher number of resistant infants in collectivist cultures. See 'Cross-cultural variations in attachment types' and the APFCC.

Q: Outline two factors that influence cross-cultural variations in attachment.

A: Childrearing practices and the different cultural norms of individualistic vs. collectivistic cultures. See 'Cross-cultural variations in attachment types' and the APFCC.

Q: Outline two effects of cross-cultural variations in attachment.

A: Higher incidence of avoidant attachment in individualistic cultures and resistant attachment in collectivistic cultures. See 'Cross-cultural variations in attachment types' and the APFCC.

Q: Describe one explanation of attachment. OR Outline two explanations of attachment.

A: Bowlby's theory, because there is more content on this and so it will be easier to gain all of the marks. See 'Explanations of attachment'. Bowlby's (Clue: innate/adaptive, crucial period, monotropy, internal working model, social releasers, and reciprocal) and the 'cupboard-love' explanations for the second question.

Q: Outline (or give two) effects of deprivation.

A: Describe the PDD model and 'affectionless psychopathy' (describe the characteristics). See 'Deprivation and privation'.

Q: Outline the (or give two) effects of privation.

A: Describe the characteristics of 'affectionless psychopathy'; this is a much more likely outcome of privation than deprivation, and its effects on cognitive or physical development. See 'Deprivation and privation' and the APFCC on privation.

Q: Outline Bowlby's maternal deprivation hypothesis.

A: Describe the hypothesis (Clue: loss of a bond means that an attachment bond did exist but is broken due to prolonged separation and once broken the bond cannot be repaired, therefore any damage such as 'affectionless psychopathy' may be permanent; but effects can be modified by good quality substitute care). See 'Deprivation and privation'.

Q: Outline two factors that influence the effects of deprivation and/or privation.

A: The length of the deprivation and the quality of the substitute care, as both of these affect bond disruption, and it is whether bond disruption occurs (deprivation) or not (privation) that distinguishes deprivation and privation. See 'Deprivation and privation' and the APFCC on privation.

Q: Outline two effects of day care. The question may specify social or cognitive, so be prepared for both.

A: Describe the negative and positive, social (sociability, peer relations, ability to form positive relationships), and cognitive (IQ achievement, language development, and age that other cognitive milestones are attained) effects. See 'Day care'.

Q: Outline two factors that influence the effects of day care on cognitive and/or social development.

A: The infant's attachment type, the quality of the day care, the type of day care, or the home environment.

EXAM TIP: In cases where you could write a lot, do keep yourself to the strict time limit of 1 minute per mark or you will lose marks elsewhere!

Comparison questions (2 + 2 + 2 marks or 3 + 3 marks)

Example exam question: Give two or three differences between...

Q: Give two differences between insecure and securely attached infants.
A: Willingness to explore their environment and responses to caregiver's departure and reunion, and the stranger.

Criticism questions (6 marks or 3 + 3 marks)

Example exam questions: Give two criticisms of...   (3 + 3 marks)
Outline one explanation and give one criticism...   (3 + 3 marks)

> **EXAM TIP**: You must be able to criticise the explanations/theories and the research/APFCCs. General criticisms in this area are:
> Ψ Much of the research is correlational. Thus, research may appear to demonstrate cause and effect, but only associations can be identified, e.g., Bowlby's research on the effect of deprivation and Ainsworth's research on attachment types, and the effects of day care.
> Ψ The ethnocentrism of the research, e.g., the Strange Situation is an imposed etic. That is, it shows a Western bias as most of the participants have been Western, white, middle-class Americans. Consequently, it may only be generalisable to the population the research was carried out on and so lacks population validity.
> Ψ The reductionism of the claim that the first attachment shapes all future relationships. This oversimplifies complex interactions to one simple explanation when there are many other factors such as later stages in childhood and the influence of peers as identified by Harris' (1997) Group Socialisation Theory.
> Ψ The determinism of the claim that the first attachment shapes all future relationships as this suggests that early attachment controls later relationships, which ignores the free will aspect, i.e., the ability of the individual to control their own behaviour.

Q: Give two criticisms of the accounts of the development of attachment.
A: Positive criticism is that validity is supported. Because the stages have face validity, they appear to be correct. However, the first asocial stage in Schaffer and Emerson's (1964) findings is contradicted by infant sociability. See 'Stages in the development of attachment'.

Q: Give two criticisms of an explanation of attachment.
A: Bowlby's theory can be criticised because the internal working model is deterministic and Schaffer and Emerson's (1964) research provides evidence against monotropy because it shows that multiple attachments can be equally important.

Q: Give two criticisms of the maternal deprivation hypothesis.
A: Positive applications of Bowlby's research to hospital practices; however, Rutter (1972) has questioned the concept of deprivation.

Q: Give two criticisms of the findings of day care.
A: Correlational criticism—can't infer cause and effect as in most research day care is not isolated as an IV, and so it cannot be said that day care causes negative/positive effects. Also, other factors are involved that modify the effects and show that the effects are subject to great variation, e.g., attachment type, quality of care, home environment. These other factors further complicate the drawing of conclusions on the effects of day care.

Example Essay Question on Day Care

Assess the extent to which day care has positive effects on cognitive and/or social development. (18 marks)

Paragraph 1: AO1

Ψ **Show you understand the question—Define day care and cognitive and social development**

Day care refers to care that is provided by people other than the parent or relatives of the infant. The issue is how day care affects the infant's primary attachments and the consequent effects on cognitive and social development. Bowlby's maternal deprivation hypothesis was used by the World Health Organisation (WHO) to predict that day care could be permanently damaging to the child's development; however, research that illustrates the positive effects of day care contradicts this.

Paragraph 2: AO2—Evidence for and evidence against

Ψ **Evidence for (positive effects)**

Research does support the argument that day care can have positive effects on cognitive and social development. For example, Andersson (1992) and Burchinal et al. (1989) found that day care children had higher IQ scores. Shea (1981) supports the positive effects on social development as this research suggests children who attend day care increase in their sociability. This is supported by Clarke-Stewart et al. (1994) who found that children who attended day care had advanced social relations. Thus, day care can enhance cognitive and social skills. However, the duration of the positive effects can be questioned as they may be short term rather than long term.

Ψ **Evidence against (negative effects)**

Contradicting the above positive effects are findings that day care can have negative effects. Recent research has suggested a negative correlation between the number of hours spent in day care and academic achievement. Belsky and Rovine (1988) suggested negative effects of day care on social development as they found that children in day care had an increased risk of having insecure attachments. Research both supports and contradicts the notion that day care has positive effects and so it might be more useful to consider the variations in the effects of day care.

Paragraph 3: AO2—Variation in the effects of day care

Ψ **Individual and social variation = multiple outcomes**

A key criticism of most of the research is that it is correlational and so cause and effect cannot be inferred. We cannot say that day care causes positive or negative effects. Also, other factors may be involved, which include the home setting, the child's attachment type, and the amount of bond disruption. For example, children who are insecurely attached may benefit more from day care than securely attached children (Egeland & Hiester, 1995). A class divide is also suggested, as children from less stimulating home environments (usually lower class) show more positive effects than children from more stimulating home environments (usually middle class). Another factor is the amount of bond disruption. Research by Clarke-Stewart et al. (1994) suggests that day care does not necessarily affect the infant/caregiver attachment. The child forms new attachments (a positive effect) but they are not as strong and do not threaten the primary attachment (hence, no negative effects). Thus, the effects of day care on cognitive and social development are subject to great variation, which means it is difficult to draw conclusions.

Conclusion: AO2

Kagan et al.'s (1980) research suggests there may be no difference between day care and home care. The effects of day care are not straightforward; there are multiple possible outcomes due to individual and social variation. For example, the effects may be fairly minimal if the child is securely attached and experiences stimulating day care; day care may have positive effects if the home environment is unstimulating; or there may be negative effects if the home environment is good and the day care is poor. For example, childminders may provide a less stimulating environment than nurseries. This means the real issue is the quality of day care, as this has the greatest influence on whether the effects are positive or not.

Attachments in Development
Essay Plans

1. To what extent are there variations in the development of attachments? (18 marks)

Paragraph 1 AO1

Define attachment and explain what is meant by the development of attachments and identify individual and cross-cultural variations.

Paragraph 2 AO2 *Evidence for*

Research evidence for variations includes studies such as Ainsworth et al. (1978) (individual differences), Ainsworth and Bell (1970), and van IJzendoorn and Kroonenberg (1988) (cross-cultural variations), as well as the temperament and maternal sensitivity hypotheses. You need to use link sentences such as: Research that illustrates cross-cultural variations…, This research supports the claim that there are variations…

Paragraph 3 AO2 *Evidence against*

Evidence that attachments are universal includes the characteristics of attachment, the stages in the development of attachment including the onset of specific attachment, and of course van IJzendoorn and Kroonenberg's research, which did show some consistency across cultures.

Concluding sentence

Weigh up the extent and focus on the question.

Individual or cultural variations may be specified. Use the above plan but omit the irrelevant content.

2. Describe and evaluate two explanations of attachments. (18 marks)

Paragraph 1 AO1

Define attachments and identify and describe two explanations, one of which should be Bowlby's, and one of the 'cupboard love' theories as these will provide lots of content.

Paragraph 2 AO2

Evaluate the 'cupboard love' theory you have selected. Use Schaffer and Emerson's (1964) and Harlow's (1959) research as evidence against 'cupboard love'. This research must be used as evaluation so *do not* describe it. Use the findings and conclusions only as evidence.

Paragraph 3 AO2

Evaluate Bowlby's theory. Consider the determinism of the internal working model—what about later relationships as suggested by Harris' (1997) Group Socialisation Theory? Schaffer and Emerson (1964) provide evidence of multiple attachments that may not be hierarchical and it is not always possible to identify which attachment is the strongest, hence this contradicts monotropy. Criticisms of the critical period, the evolutionary basis of and determinism of Bowlby's theory could also be included.

Concluding sentence

Whilst both theories have negative criticisms they have made important contributions to our understanding…

3. Consider whether research studies support the view that maternal deprivation/privation can have long-term effects. (18 marks)

Paragraph 1 AO1/AO2

Define and describe the maternal deprivation hypothesis, e.g., the effects of deprivation as a consequence of separation. If prolonged the existing attachment bond may be broken, which is particularly likely to have negative effects if it takes place within the critical period. Such effects can be permanent, as once broken the bond cannot be repaired, i.e., affectionless psychopathy. Distinguish between separation, deprivation, and privation using Rutter's (1981) criticism. Explain that separation is usually temporary and so has no bond disruption, but that it becomes deprivation when there is bond disruption due to the length or nature of the separation. Thus, in assessing the effects of deprivation, privation must also be considered, as research does not always clearly distinguish between the two. For example, some of the sample in Bowlby's 'forty-four juvenile thieves' experienced deprivation, and others privation.

Paragraph 2 AO2 *Evidence for*

Research evidence: Bowlby (1946) and his follow-up research in the TB clinic (Bowlby et al.,1956), Spitz and Wolf (1946), Goldfarb (1947), Douglas (1975), and Quinton and Rutter (1976). Remember this is AO2 so don't describe the research, rather use it as evaluation, i.e., This supports...

Paragraph 3 AO2 *Evidence against*

The developmental retardation may be due to a lack of stimulation not just maternal care, although Widdowson (1951) does support the importance of emotional care. Research is correlational, and so other factors may be involved as Clarke and Clarke (1976) suggest, and as Rutter et al.'s (1976) research on the Isle of Wight illustrates. Also, Bowlby's research may be biased and the case study method lacks generalisability. Thus, the findings may lack validity and therefore meaning, and so may not be evidence of long-term effects. The critical period has also been criticised and Hodges and Tizard's (1989) research supports this criticism, as institutionalised children did form attachments after the age of 4 years. Thus, a sensitive period rather than a critical period may be more accurate. Bowlby et al.'s (1956) research in the TB clinic showed that the effects of deprivation can be overcome to some extent. The research demonstrates the importance of the substitute care in minimising bond disruption. Also, experiences in middle and later childhood are just as important as early childhood (Clarke & Clarke, 1976). Thus, long-term effects are not inevitable.

Conclusion AO2

Research does evidence long-term effects of deprivation/privation but some of these effects can be reversed, as Bowlby et al.'s (1956) study in the TB clinic identified that the effects depend on the amount of bond disruption and, as Hodges and Tizard's research suggests, the quality of subsequent care. However, the research on effects is correlational, causation cannot be inferred, and other factors may be involved. In reality there are multiple outcomes that also depend on situational factors and the characteristics of the individual.

4. Consider what research (theories and/or studies) into deprivation/privation has told us about the reversibility/irreversibility of deprivation/privation.   (18 marks)

Same as above but the link sentence must include the word reversible.

5. Consider the extent to which Bowlby has contributed to our understanding of attachments.   (18 marks)

Paragraph 1 AO1

Define attachment and outline Bowlby's theory of attachment and maternal deprivation hypothesis to explain what his contributions were.

Paragraph 2 AO2 *Evidence for*

Assess the positive implications of Bowlby's work for child-care practices. Discuss the fact that his research has stimulated much further research in this area and how he worked closely with Mary Ainsworth to make significant contributions to our understanding of infant development. Thus, he drew from Ainsworth, Freud, and evolutionary theory, and he stimulated research that drew from his findings. Then there is the issue of validity and also the meaningfulness of his findings as, if they lack validity, his contribution must be limited.

Paragraph 3 AO2 *Evidence against*

Include criticisms of the validity of Bowlby's work and criticisms of his theory of attachment and the maternal deprivation hypothesis, including the fact that it suited the political agenda and so was incorporated into post World War 2 'propaganda'. Discuss the guilt this has caused generations of women, and the fact that there is much research that directly contradicts his claim that separation through day care would cause long-lasting damage, i.e., draw from the research evidence on day care.

Concluding sentence

Weigh up the extent, e.g., It is difficult to quantify, but Bowlby's work was highly influential in spite of the criticisms made of it and so...

6. Assess the extent to which psychological research (theories and/
or studies) supports the view that day care can have positive
effects on social development. (18 marks)

Paragraph 1 AO1

Define and describe what day care and social development are. Identify different types of day care (nurseries, childminders, nannies, crèches).

Paragraph 2 AO2 *Evidence for*

This should include research evidence on the positive effects on social development. Remember to use link sentences to make this AO2. For example, research by Shea (1981), Clarke-Stewart et al. (1994), and Roggman et al. (1994) supports the positive effects of day care on social development. Remember, focus on findings/conclusions; any other aspects of the research are irrelevant AO1.

Paragraph 3 AO2 *Evidence against*

Include research evidence on the negative effects on social development. For example, Pennebaker et al. (1981), Belsky and Rovine (1988), and Sroufe (1983) contradicted the idea that day care has positive effects.

Conclusion AO2

Also, as the evidence is correlational, causation cannot be inferred and so we cannot say that day care has positive effects as only associations can be inferred. Furthermore, any effects are modified by individual differences in attachment type, the level of stimulation in the home environment, and the type and quality of day care, which must all be taken into account when trying to 'weigh up' the conclusion. There are multiple outcomes of day care, which means it is difficult to draw conclusions, but given the evidence that day care can be positive, then the focus should be on transferring this to cases where day care still has negative effects.

If the question had asked you to consider negative effects then you would simply reverse the order of paragraphs 2 and 3. Also see 'Example essay question on day care'.

7. Assess the extent to which psychological research (theories and/
or studies) supports the view that day care can have positive effects
on cognitive development. (18 marks)

Paragraph 1 AO1

Describe what day care and cognitive development are. Identify different types of day care (nurseries, childminders, nannies, crèches).

Paragraph 2 AO2 *Evidence for*

This should include research evidence on the positive effects on cognitive development. Remember to use link sentences to make this AO2. For example, Operation Headstart, Burchinal et al. (1989), Broberg et al. (1997), and Andersson et al. (1992) all support positive effects of day care on cognitive development.

Paragraph 3 AO2 *Evidence against*

This should include research evidence on the negative effects on cognitive development. For example, Tizard's (1979) research on conversational differences contradicts positive effects, and Clarke Stewart et al. (1994) claimed that longer than 6 hours per day had negative effects. However, there is considerably less evidence against than for positive effects.

Conclusion AO2

Also, as the evidence is correlational, causation cannot be inferred and so we cannot say that day care has positive effects as only associations can be inferred. Furthermore, any effects are modified by individual differences in attachment type, the level of stimulation in the home environment, and the type and quality of day care, which must all be taken into account when trying to 'weigh up' the conclusion. There are multiple outcomes of day care, which means it is difficult to draw conclusions, but given the evidence that day care can be positive, then the focus should be on transferring this to cases where day care still has negative effects.

If the question had asked you to consider negative effects then you would simply reverse the order of paragraphs 2 and 3. Also see 'Example essay question on day care'.

Attachments in Development Crib Sheets

Cross-reference with Brody and Dwyer's revision guide, the attachments in development APFCCs, findings/conclusions (in the Appendices), essay plans, and AO1 revision summary.

Definitions

Attachment: ....

....

Secure attachment: ....

....

Insecure attachment: ....

....

Cross-cultural variations in attachment: ....

....

Privation: ....

....

Cognitive development: ....

....

Social development: ....

....

Day care: ....

....

Characteristics of attachments

Separation distress: ....

Stranger anxiety: ....

Reunion behaviour: ....

Seeking proximity: ....

The development of attachments, i.e., the stages

Schaffer and Emerson (1964): ....

1. Asocial stage: ....

2. Indiscriminate stage: ....

3. Specific attachments (and subsequently multiple attachments):..

....

Validity: ....

....

Infant sociability: ....

....

Explanations of attachment

Psychodynamic theory: AO1: ....

....

AO2: ....

....

Learning theories: AO1: ....

....

....

AO2: ....

....

Bowlby: ....

....

Innate/survival: ....

....

Critical period: ....

....

Internal working model: ....

....

Monotropy: ....

....

Reciprocal: ....

....

AO2: ....

Individual variation in attachments (Ainsworth and Bell)

The Strange Situation: ....

Type A: ....

Type B: ....

Type C: ....

Evaluation of the Strange Situation

Type D: ....

Imposed etic: ....

Question validity: ....

Is attachment a stable characteristic? ....

Cross-cultural variations (van IJzendoorn & Kroonenberg)

Individualistic vs. collectivistic: ....

AO2: Universality: ....

Variation within cultures is 1½ times greater than between: ....
....

Deprivation and privation

PDD model (Robertson & Bowlby): ....
....

AO2: ....
....

The maternal deprivation hypothesis: ....
....

AO2: ....
....

Privation: ....
....

AO2: Are the effects reversible? ....
....

Distinguish between separation, deprivation, and privation:..
....

Day care—include research evidence

Positive effects on social development: ....
....

Negative effects on social development: ....
....

Positive effects on cognitive development: ....
....

Negative effects on cognitive development: ....
....

Improving day care

Consistency and quality: ....
....

AO2 correlational evidence: ....

Variation: ....

Stress Learning Objectives

On completion of this topic you should be familiar with the following.

Stress as a bodily response

* Define stress and describe the body's response to stress, e.g., the sympatho-adrenomedullary (SAM) axis and the hypothalamic-pituitary-adrenal (HPA) axis.
* Evaluate the physiological response to stress.
* Define, outline, and evaluate the General Adaptation Syndrome (GAS).
* Describe and assess the relationship between stress and physical illness, including cardiovascular disorders and the effect of stress on the immune system.
* Define the terms cardiovascular disorders and the immune system.
* Describe the Aims, Procedures, Findings, Conclusions, and Criticisms (APFCC) of a study on the effect of stress on the immune system, e.g., Kiecolt-Glaser et al.'s (1995) 'wound healing as evidence of immunosuppression', and stress and coronary heart disease, e.g., Friedman and Rosenman's (1959, 1974) 'Type A/B behaviour pattern'.

Sources of stress

* Define stressor and identify and analyse sources of stress, including life changes and workplace stressors, and be able to define these terms.
* Describe the APFCC for a study of life changes, e.g., Rahe et al.'s (1970) 'life events scale' and a study of workplace stress, e.g., Marmot et al.'s (1997) 'hierarchy and control'.
* Outline and evaluate the individual differences that modify the effects of stress, including personality (e.g., Type A/B, 'hardy' personality), and gender (e.g., hormones, socialised roles).

Critical issue—Stress management

* Define the terms stress management, physiological approaches to stress management, and psychological approaches to stress management.
* Describe and assess the strengths and weaknesses of physiological and psychological stress management techniques.

Cross-reference the above learning objectives with the Specification and fill in the self-assessment box below on completion of the topic.

SELF-ASSESSMENT BOX

☺ **Which of the above do you know?**

☹ **Are there any gaps in your knowledge that need to be targeted during revision?**

The Body's Response to Stressors

For details, see Eysenck's textbook (page 137) and Brody and Dwyer's revision guide (page 68).

Definition of stress

Imagine that you are experiencing a stressful situation, e.g., making a speech in front of a large audience, taking a driving test, or sitting an examination. What changes happen within your body when you are stressed? Read about the role of the autonomic nervous system and summarise what happens by filling in the blanks in the diagram below making sure you have included the following terms:

Hypothalamus	Pituitary gland	Corticosteroids
Adrenaline	Adrenal medulla	ACTH
Adrenal cortex	Noradrenaline	Sympathetic branch of the ANS

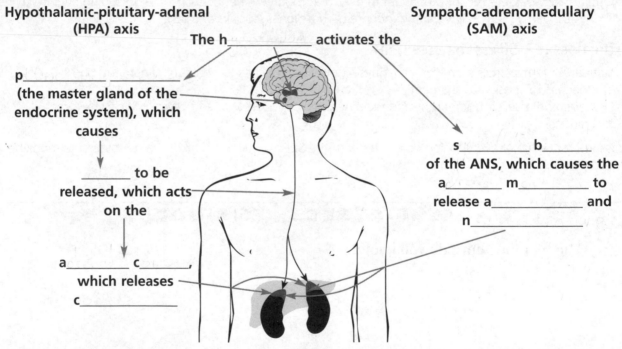

Hypothalamic-pituitary-adrenal (HPA) axis

The h_____ activates the

p_____ _____ (the master gland of the endocrine system), which causes

_____ to be released, which acts on the

a_____ c_____, which releases

c_____

Sympatho-adrenomedullary (SAM) axis

s_____ b_____ of the ANS, which causes the a_____ m_____ to release a_____ and n_____

Now add onto the diagram the effects of 1) the immediate 'fight or flight' response due to arousal of the sympathetic branch of the ANS (the sympatho-adrenomedullary axis), e.g., faster breathing and pulse, etc., and 2) the longer term stress response of the hypothalamic-pituitary-adrenal axis, e.g., release of cortisol, etc.

Using this in the exam

AO1 questions:

Explain what is meant by the terms stress and stressor (3 + 3 marks)

Outline two ways in which the body responds to stress. (3 + 3 marks)

Essay question:

To what extent is the stress response physiological? (18 marks)

The content on this worksheet could be used as AO1 and evidence for (AO2) the physiological basis of the stress response. The evaluation on the next worksheet could be used as evidence against.

The General Adaptation Syndrome

For details, see Eysenck's textbook (page 142) and Brody and Dwyer's revision guide (page 71). Fill in the gaps using the letter clues provided and use the cues in the table to guide your note taking.

The General Adaptation Syndrome (GAS) was put forward by Selye (1936). Based on his work with r_____, and later hospital patients, Selye predicted a n___-s_____ response to a stressor. He believed that the body shows the same p_____ of response to all s_____ and that the non-specific response consists of t_____ stages.

Definition of the General Adaptation Syndrome (Selye, 1936)
The three stages of GAS ARE (note the mnemonic)
Stage 1: <u>A</u>larm reaction
Stage 2: <u>R</u>esistance
Stage 3: <u>E</u>xhaustion

Evaluation of GAS

Ψ Positive implications of Selye's (1936) work.

Ψ Different stressors have different responses, and so there is not a single passive response.

Ψ Extrapolation of animal research to humans.

Evaluation of the physiological approach to stress

Ψ The role of self-perception means that individuals interpret stress in different ways and so their physiological responses differ.

Ψ GAS ignores the individual differences that characterise humans, e.g., gender, personality, culture, and differences in physiological reactivity.

Ψ GAS ignores psychological factors, e.g., differences in cognitive, emotional, and behavioural responses OR ABC, <u>A</u>ffect, <u>B</u>ehaviour, and <u>C</u>ognition.

Conclusions

The advantage of measuring only the p_____ responses to s_____ is that ob_____ m_____ is possible. However, this ignores the considerable v_____ in the experience of stress as a result of i_____ d_____ in self-perception, physiological reactivity, and other factors such as p_____, g_____, and c_____, which can modify the experience of stress. Thus, the physiological basis to the stress response is unquestionable. However, it is less clear how the ph_____ interacts with the ps_____, as on the one hand one might say a stressful personality determines the physiological stress response, but on the other hand personality may be a consequence of physiological reactivity levels. It is most likely that the experience of stress is due to a complex i_____ of physiological and psychological factors. This is a more comprehensive approach to the stress response as considering it only as a physiological mechanism is r_____t (oversimplified) because it reduces a complex response to a single response (physiology) and is also physiologically d_____tic, that is it ignores the f_____ will of the individual to take control of their own behaviour.

Using this in the exam

AO1 questions:

Explain what is meant by the terms General Adaptation Syndrome and stress. (3 + 3 marks)
Outline the main features of Selye's General Adaptation Syndrome. (6 marks)
Give two criticisms of Selye's General Adaptation Syndrome. (3 + 3 marks)

Essay questions:

Consider the extent to which the stress response is physiological. (18 marks)
GAS is evidence for, and describing this and the hypothalamic-pituitary-adrenal axis and the sympatho-adrenomedullary axis will provide AO1 content. The evaluation on this worksheet is evidence against.
Assess the contributions of Selye to our understanding of stress. (18 marks)

Stress and Physical Illness

For details, see Eysenck's textbook (page 144) and Brody and Dwyer (page 72). Fill in the gaps using the letter clues provided and use the cues in the table to guide your note taking.

The e_____ stage of GAS demonstrates the role of stress in physical illness. There are two ways in which stress can cause illness:

Ψ   Directly:
Ψ   Indirectly:

Curtis (2000) has linked stress with a range of physical illnesses including, h_____s, inf_____ i_____, car_____ d_____, di_____, a_____a, and r_____d a_____s.

You could also be asked an APFCC question on this so please complete the APFCCs for a study of stress and the immune system and stress and cardiovascular disorders.

Definition of cardiovascular disorders
Stress and hypertension Ψ Raised blood pressure can damage the blood vessels.
Stress and coronary heart disease (CHD) Ψ The damage caused by hypertension begins the process of arteriosclerosis (thickening of the arteries).
Definition of the immune system
Stress and the immune system Ψ Direct effects—stress decreases the number of white blood cells, known as immunosuppression.

Evaluation of the relationship between stress and physical illness

Ψ There is strong evidence that supports the link between stress and illness.

Ψ Evidence is inconclusive (Bachen, Cohen, & Marsland, 1997).

Ψ Functioning of the immune system of stressed individuals falls within the normal range.

Ψ Measurements of stress and the immune system may lack reliability and validity as the immune system is very complex and so difficult to assess.

Ψ Ignores individual differences.

Ψ Ignores psychological factors.

Conclusions

There is strong e_____ that links stress to illness. However, most of this evidence is based on natural e_____ or it is c_____al evidence. Consequently, c_____ and e_____ cannot be inferred: we cannot say that stress causes illness but can only say that it is a_____d with illness. Another methodological weakness of this research is the likelihood that o_____ f_____ are involved, such as l_____e, i_____ differences, and coping ability. Thus, individuals with a less stressful personality type (e.g., Type B or hardy personality) may be less v_____ to stress-related illness. To conclude, the relationship between s_____ and i_____ is highly complex and so caution should be taken when considering the direct effect of stress on illness. The stress response is not just physiological and so it is oversimplistic and red_____ to consider the relationship between stress and illness as purely physical. There are important ps_____ factors that mediate in this relationship.

Using this in the exam

AO1 questions:

Explain what is meant by the terms cardiovascular disorders and the immune system. (3 + 3 marks)

Describe the APFCC of one study into the effects of stress on the cardiovascular system OR the immune system OR that has investigated stress and physical illness. (6 marks)

Explain two factors that can influence stress and physical illness. (3 + 3 marks)
For example, any two: individual differences such as personality (hardy personalities may be less susceptible) and lifestyle, including stress management techniques.

Essay question:

Consider the extent to which research (theories and/or studies) shows a relationship between stress and illness. (18 marks)

Sources of Stress

For details, see Eysenck's textbook (page 153) and Brody and Dwyer's revision guide (page 76). Fill in the gaps using the letter clues provided and use the cues in the table to guide your note taking.

Sources of stress are factors that c_____ stress. You need to know about l_____ ch_____ and wo_____ s_____ for the exam (which is another source of stress!).

You could also be asked an APFCC question on this so please complete the APFCCs on life changes and workplace stressors as two sources of stress.

Life events—Holmes and Rahe (1967)
Ψ Changes absorb 'psychic energy'.
Ψ Social Readjustment Rating Scale (SRRS)—43 life events.
Ψ A weak correlation between life change units (LCUs) and illness.
Evaluation of the SRRS evidence
Ψ Evidence is correlational.
Ψ There are individual differences in self-perception of the events.
Ψ Self-report method is retrospective and may be biased by participant reactivity.
Ψ Daily hassles are more representative of real-life stress (DeLongis et al., 1982).

Pressures of work

Ψ Predictability and controllability—a curvilinear relationship:
  - Glass et al.'s (1969) noise experiment.

  - Brady's (1958) 'executive monkeys' study.

  - Marmot et al.'s (1997) 'hierarchy and control in the civil service'.

  - Internal/external locus of control (Rotter, 1966). How can this be linked to workplace stress?

Ψ Role conflict (Margolis & Kroes, 1974).

Ψ Burnout (Maslach & Jackson, 1982).

Using this in the exam

AO1 questions:

Explain what is meant by the terms life changes and workplace stressor. (3 + 3 marks)

Describe the APFCC of a study that has investigated life changes/a workplace stressor as
a source of stress. (6 marks)

Essay questions:

Outline and evaluate research (theories and/or studies) into life changes as a source of stress. (18 marks)

Outline and evaluate research (theories and/or studies) into the workplace as a source of stress. (18 marks)

Evidence for: describe and evaluate the research evidence for life changes or workplace stressors. Evidence against: consider alternative sources of stress methodological criticisms, e.g., correlational evidence and the fact that experience of any stressor is modified by self-perception and individual differences.

Individual Differences and Stress

For details, see Eysenck's textbook (page 162) and Brody and Dwyer's revision guide (page 79). Fill in the gaps using the letter clues provided and use the cues in the table to guide your note taking.

Failing to account for i_____ d_____ is a key criticism of attempts to identify the physiological e_____ of stress and the m_____ of stress. Individual differences refers to differences in p_____ and g_____.

Personality
Ψ Personality types: A, B, C (Friedman & Rosenman, 1959):
• Type As.
• Type Bs.
• Type Cs.
Ψ Hardiness (Kobasa, 1979): Hardy individuals are better able to cope with stress because of certain characteristics (remember the 3 Cs):
• Commitment.
• Challenge.
• Control.

Evaluation of the relationship between personality and stress

Ψ Cause and effect—is personality a cause or effect of stress?

Ψ Do you think you have a stable personality type? Classification is vastly oversimplified, which has led to other types being suggested to expand the type A/B behaviour pattern.

Gender

Ψ Males respond more strenuously to stressors (Stoney, David, & Matthews, 1987).

Ψ Biological differences—the calming effect of women's hormones! Oestrogen and oxytocin, the 'tend and befriend' response.

Ψ Psychological differences, i.e., gender socialisation has led to women engaging in fewer unhealthy behaviours, e.g., less risk-taking behaviour. Also, there are significant differences in social support—women have more friends!

Evaluation of the relationship between gender and stress

Ψ Is the gender difference in stress biological or psychological?

Ψ Differences may be as great within genders as between genders.

Ψ Research is a product of time and context and is therefore biased.

Ψ Gender differences are blurring due to the changing role of women, e.g., the dual-burden may mean that women are becoming the more stressed sex.

Conclusions

I_____ differences m_____y the effects of stressors. This means different people experience the same stressor in different ways. The b_____ response to stress is fairly con_____ across individuals. However, self-p_____ and in_____n are not, and as these can trigger the body's response, then the stress response is not a non-specific behaviour as suggested by S_____. Thus, stress is a unique experience specific to the individual and it may be influenced by the p_____ and gender of the person concerned.

Using this in the exam

AO1 questions:

Outline two factors that can modify the effects of stressors. (3 + 3 marks)

Outline two ways in which personality can modify the effects of stressors OR gender. (6 marks)

Essay question:

Consider the extent to which stressors have been shown to be modified by gender and/or personality. (18 marks)

Also, individual differences is key AO2 in any essay question as they show that stress is not solely a physiological response, that sources of stress are not objective, and that the success of stress management methods may depend on individual differences.

Stress Management

For details, see Eysenck's textbook (page 171) and Brody and Dwyer's revision guide (page 81). Fill in the gaps using the letter clues provided and use the cues in the table to guide your note taking.

Stress m_____ is an important application given the incidence of stress-related i_____ in contemporary society. It is estimated that people have 10+ days of stress-related illness off per year! How do you c____ when you're stressed? One of the key aspects of stress management is increasing one's s___-e_____, that is increasing one's sense of c_____l. The definition of stress clarifies this as it shows that to decrease stress we must match our p_____n of c_____ a_____ to our perception of the de_____ of the s_____.

Physiological methods

Biofeedback

Ψ How the technique works.

Ψ Research evidence for biofeedback (Budzynski et al., 1973, and Curtis, 2000).

Evaluation

Ψ Relaxation or biofeedback? Difficulties in interpretation.

Ψ Sense of control or physiological mechanisms?

Ψ Individual differences, e.g., it works well with children.

Anti-anxiety drugs
Ψ Control the body's response to stress, e.g., beta blockers, benzodiazepines, buspirone.

Evaluation
Ψ Effectively reduce physiological arousal.

Ψ Deal with symptoms not causes of stress.

Ψ Side effects.

Psychological methods

Stress inoculation training (Meichenbaum, 1977, 1985)

There are three main phases to stress inoculation training, which should be introduced before the individual becomes too anxious or depressed. Remember the initials <u>ASA</u> to cue your recall.

Ψ <u>A</u>ssessment.

Ψ <u>S</u>tress reduction techniques.

Ψ <u>A</u>pplication and follow-through.

Ψ Plus research evidence/empirical support (Meichenbaum, 1977).

Evaluation

Ψ It is effective because it increases sense of control and self-efficacy.

Ψ Individual differences in ability to use the technique.

Ψ Less effective in highly stressful situations.

Hardiness training

Ψ 'Hardy' individuals cope better with stress. List their characteristics.

Ψ Hardiness training involves three techniques (remember the initials <u>FRC</u> as a cue):

- <u>F</u>_____g.

- <u>R</u>_____ st_____ sit_____.

- <u>C</u>om_____ through s_____-i_____t.

Evaluation

Ψ Sarafino (1990).

Ψ Sample bias and so generalisability is questionable.

Ψ Correlational evidence.

Using this in the exam

AO1 questions:

Describe <u>one/two</u> <u>physiological/psychological</u> approaches to stress management.　　(6 marks or 3 + 3 marks)
Give one strength and one weakness of one <u>physiological/psychological</u>
approach to stress management.　　(3 + 3 marks)
Outline two factors that influence the effectiveness of stress management.　　(3 + 3 marks)
For example, self-perception and control.

Essay questions:

Outline and evaluate <u>physiological/psychological</u> approaches to stress management.　　(18 marks)
Consider the effectiveness of <u>physiological/psychological</u> approaches to stress management.　　(18 marks)

EXAM TIP: Underlined parts mean it could be either of the two words.

Stress APFCCs

Wound healing as evidence of immunosuppression—Kiecolt-Glaser et al.'s (1995) study of the effect of stress on the immune system

Aims:

Procedures:

Findings:

Conclusions:

Criticisms:

Type A/B behaviour pattern—Friedman and Rosenman's (1959, 1974) study of the relationship between stress and coronary heart disease

Aims:

Procedures:

Findings:

Conclusions:

Criticisms:

Life events scale (SRRS)—Rahe et al.'s (1970) study of life changes as a source of stress

Aims:

Procedures:

Findings:

Conclusions:

Criticisms:

Hierarchy and control—Marmot et al.'s (1997) study of workplace stress

Aims:

Procedures:

Findings:

Conclusions:

Criticisms:

Stress Revision AO1

Use this as a checklist, i.e., tick off when you feel confident you can answer the following questions and/or have prepared a model answer for each type of question. The range of potential exam questions is finite so you can prepare for all possibilities.

Definition questions (2 + 2 + 2 marks or 3 + 3 marks)

You may be asked to define any of the terms that appear on the Specification, except for those that are given as examples. So cross-reference with the Specification.

EXAM TIP: If you have not included enough content to access all of the marks, give an example.

Stress	Stressor	General Adaptation Syndrome (GAS)
Immune system	Cardiovascular disorders	Workplace stressor
Life changes	Stress management	
Physiological approaches to stress management		Psychological approaches to stress management

Definitions

Cross-reference with the glossary in the Brody and Dwyer revision guide (pages 193–202).

Example exam question: What is meant by the terms… *[and two or three of the following would be stated]*

Stress:

Stressor:

General Adaptation Syndrome (GAS):

Immune system:

Cardiovascular disorders:

Workplace stressor:

Life changes:

Stress management:

Physiological approaches to stress management:

Psychological approaches to stress management:

Research questions (6 marks or 3 + 3 marks)

Cross-reference with the completed APFCCs in the appendix of the Brody and Dwyer revision guide (pages 185–188).

Example exam questions: Describe the aims/procedures/findings/conclusions/one criticism of a study into... *[any two aspects could be specified]* (6 marks)
Describe the findings of research into... (6 marks)
Describe the conclusions of research into... (6 marks)
Give two criticisms of research into... (3 + 3 marks)

> **EXAM TIP**: The question may ask for any two APFCCs or may just ask for *findings*, *conclusions*, or *two criticisms*. So be prepared to give enough detail for 6 marks on the findings or conclusions and know two criticisms for all studies in sufficient detail for 3 marks each.

You must be able to give the APFCCs for the following stress studies:

Q: Describe the APFCC of one study into the effects of stress on the immune system. OR findings/conclusions.
A: Kiecolt-Glaser et al.'s (1995) 'wound healing as evidence of immunosuppression', and Cohen et al. (1991), and Kiecolt-Glaser (1984) if findings/conclusions.

Q: Describe the APFCC of one study into the relationship between stress and cardiovascular disorders. OR findings/conclusions.
A: Friedman and Rosenman's (1959,1974) 'Type A/B behaviour pattern', Ganster et al. (1991), and Matthews et al. (1977) if findings/conclusions.

Q: Describe the APFCC of one study into stress and physical illness. OR findings/conclusions.
A: Either Friedman and Rosenman (1959,1974), or Kiecolt-Glaser et al. (1984). Both for findings/conclusions.

Q: Describe the APFCC of one study that has investigated life changes as a source of stress. OR findings/conclusions.
A: Rahe et al.'s (1970) 'life events as measured by the SRRS', Holmes and Rahe (1967), and Rahe and Arthur (1977) if findings/conclusions.

Q: Describe the APFCC of one study that has investigated workplace stressors. OR findings/conclusions.
A: Marmot et al.'s (1997) 'workplace stress and stress-related illness', and Shirom (1989), and/or Margolis and Kroes (1974) if findings/conclusions.

Q: Describe the APFCC of one study into sources of stress. OR findings/conclusions.
A: Either Rahe et al. (1970), or Marmot et al. (1997). Both for findings/conclusions.

These are only suggestions, so use other studies if you prefer.

Explanations/theories questions (3 + 3 marks or 6 marks)

These questions could be worded in a number of ways.

Example exam questions: Describe one explanation of... (6 marks)
Outline two explanations of... (3 + 3 marks)
Describe one explanation and give one criticism of... (3 + 3 marks)
Outline the main features of... (6 marks)
Outline two factors that explain... (3 + 3 marks)
Outline two factors that influence... (3 + 3 marks)
Outline two ways that... (3 + 3 marks)
Outline two effects of... (3 + 3 marks)

Q: Outline two ways the body responds to stressors. OR Outline two effects of stress on the body.

A: The dual-stress response: hypothalamic-pituitary-adrenal axis, or the General Adaptation Syndrome (GAS). See 'The body's response to stressors' and 'The General Adaptation Syndrome'.

Q: Outline the main features of Selye's General Adaptation Syndrome.

A: Describe the three stages (ARE = mnemonic): alarm reaction, resistance, and exhaustion. See 'The General Adaptation Syndrome'.

Q: Outline the effects of stress on the immune system.

A: Describe immunosuppression. See 'Stress and physical illness' and the APFCC.

Q: Outline the relationship between stress and cardiovascular disorders.

A: Describe the effects of heightened blood pressure, release of sugar for energy, and the consequent thickening of the arteries (atherosclerosis). See 'Stress and physical illness' and the APFCC.

Q: Outline the relationship between stress and physical illness.

A: Describe the HPA axis and immunosuppression and/or the 'fight or flight' response and cardiovascular disorders. See 'Stress and physical illness' and the APFCCs. Also, explain that the exhaustion stage of the GAS is linked to physical illness.

Q: Outline two (or one) sources of stress.

A: Life changes and/or workplace stress. See 'Sources of stress' and the APFCCs.

Q: Outline two ways that life changes may cause stress.

A: Describe how life changes absorb 'psychic energy' and require psychological adjustment. See 'Sources of stress' and the APFCC.

Q: Outline two ways the workplace may cause stress.

A: Control and interpersonal relationships. See 'Sources of stress' and the APFCC.

Q: Outline two factors that can modify the effects of stress.

A: Describe gender or personality differences that are covered in 'Individual differences and stress'.

Q: Outline two ways that personality or gender may modify the effects of stressors.

A: Describe gender or personality differences depending on what is specified in the question. See 'Individual differences and stress'.

Q: Describe one physiological approach to stress management.

A: Biofeedback or anti-anxiety drugs. See 'Stress management'.

Q: Describe one psychological approach to stress management.

A: Stress inoculation training or hardiness training. See 'Stress management'.

Q: Outline one method of stress management.

A: Select either biofeedback or anti-anxiety drugs or stress inoculation training or hardiness training. See 'Stress management'.

EXAM TIP: Any question that asks you to 'explain two factors that influence...' [e.g., the physiological response to stress, the effects of a stressor, the relationship between stress and illness, stress management methods] can all be answered in the same way. Describe the role of self-perception as explained by the transactional model and how individual differences modify the experience of stress.

Criticism questions (3 + 3 marks)

Example exam questions: Give two criticisms of...   (3 + 3 marks)

Outline one explanation and give one criticism...   (3 + 3 marks)

EXAM TIP: Evaluation questions usually ask for two criticisms, so make sure you have prepared two for each of the APFCCs and the above explanations/theories questions. Some criticisms apply to most areas, for example:

Ψ Correlational research does not prove cause and effect. Thus, even though the variables of stress and illness are associated, it cannot be concluded that stress causes illness. Furthermore, there may be other factors influencing the two variables such as lifestyle and individual differences.

Ψ Self-report method: studies like those of Friedman and Rosenman (1959, 1974) and Holmes and Rahe (1967) rely on this method, which is biased because the materials may give rise to demand characteristics and this could lead to participant reactivity. Thus, evaluation apprehension and the social desirability effect may distort the findings.

Ψ Individual differences: used as criticism of Selye's GAS and just about everything! The perception of stress and reaction to it are so varied. Personality and gender differences are rarely accounted for by research.

Q: Give two criticisms of stress as a physiological response.

A: It ignores psychological factors and individual differences. See 'The General Adaptation Syndrome'.

Q: Give two criticisms of Selye's General Adaptation Syndrome.

A: The non-specific response can be questioned as there are individual differences and the extrapolation from animal research can be criticised. See 'The General Adaptation Syndrome'.

Q: Give two criticisms of the assumption that stress causes illness (or the immune system or cardiovascular disorders may be specified).

A: Correlational and natural experiment evidence means that causation cannot be inferred and other factors may be involved, e.g., psychological factors can modify the effect of stress. See 'Stress and physical illness' and the APFCCs.

Q: Give two criticisms of life changes (or workplace stressors) as a source of stress.

A: You are only as stressed if you perceive yourself to be and so these stressors may be experienced as a threat or a challenge depending on the individual's self-perception. Also, these sources do not take into account individual differences.

Q: Give two criticisms of the assumption that individual differences (personality or gender may be specified) modify the effects of stressors.

A: Cause and effect cannot be inferred and other factors may be implicated in the effect as the research is correlational.

Q: Give one strength and one weakness of a physiological/psychological approach to stress management.

A: Choose between drugs and biofeedback or stress inoculation training or hardiness training, depending on whether physiological or psychological is specified in the question. See 'Stress management' and 'Example essay question on stress management', which evaluates the approaches.

Q: Outline one strength and one weakness of one method of stress management.

A: Select either biofeedback, anti-anxiety drugs, stress inoculation training, or hardiness training. See 'Stress management' and 'Example essay question on stress management', which evaluates the approaches.

Example Essay Question on Stress Management

Consider the effectiveness of physiological approaches to stress management. (18 marks)

Paragraph 1: AO1 and AO2—Description and evaluation of anti-anxiety drugs

Physiological approaches to stress are techniques that try to control the body's response to stress by reducing physiological reactivity.

Ψ Anti-anxiety drugs

Anti-anxiety drugs decrease the 'fight or flight' response such as high blood pressure, increased pulse, and so on by acting upon the CNS and ANS; beta blockers, benzodiazepines, and buspirone may be used. However, there are issues of dependence (physical and psychological), tolerance, and side effects. They are effective in relieving the unpleasant physiological effects of stress and so are often a useful short-term strategy, which enables the individual to achieve a state where psychological intervention can be introduced. Furthermore, the most recently introduced anti-anxiety drug—buspirone—has considerably less side effects and no withdrawal symptoms and so provides a 'safer' option than the earlier drugs.

Paragraph 2: AO1 and AO2—Description and evaluation of biofeedback

Ψ Biofeedback

Biofeedback works by training the participants to recognise their heightened physiological reactivity and reduce it through relaxation exercises. The biofeedback machine provides either auditory or visual feedback to indicate high physiological arousal. The patient then uses relaxation techniques to reduce the arousal and is rewarded by the subsequent feedback, which indicates a drop in arousal. Thus, the machine uses the learning principles of operant conditioning, as the feedback is a form of positive reinforcement. Biofeedback lacks ecological validity, as it cannot be used in other settings because of the machinery involved. Also, it is questionable whether it is the biofeedback that decreases stress or the relaxation techniques that accompany it. However, it has been found to be effective in treating people with generalised anxiety disorder as a consequence of stress and it is considered particularly effective with children, who tend to treat it as a game.

Ψ Deals with symptoms (effects in the body) rather than causes

Both techniques are reductionist because they only focus on the effects of stress, not the underlying causes.

Paragraph 3: AO2—Commentary on the effectiveness of the physiological approach

Ψ Factors that modify the effectiveness of stress management techniques

The effectiveness of physiological approaches can be affected by other factors and the main criticism of the physiological approaches is that they ignore these other factors. They do not take into account psychological factors in the stress response, such as underlying emotions and cognitions. The importance of psychological factors is illustrated by the fact that individual differences can modify the effectiveness of stress management techniques. For example, gender and cultural differences in social support have been suggested, which act as a 'buffer' against stress and so interact with the effectiveness of the physiological approaches. Also, individual differences in perceived ability to cope (transactional model) may influence the effectiveness of a technique as the individual's perceived self-efficacy and belief in the technique will be influential. Thus, cognition plays an important role in stress management and so it is a significant weakness that the physiological approaches ignore this.

Conclusion: AO2

The effectiveness of physiological approaches is unquestionable in that they do 'work' in terms of reducing the body's response to stress. However, it is unlikely that they even begin to treat the real causes of the stress. Their greatest drawback is that they only work on one level—the physiological level—when a complex response like stress must also be dealt with at the cognitive, emotional, and behavioural levels. Thus, the physiological approach alone is reductionist (oversimplified) and can only be truly effective if combined in a multi-perspective approach to stress management.

Stress Essay Plans

1. Outline and evaluate the physiological responses to stress. (18 marks)

Paragraph 1 AO1

Define stress and outline the dual stress response, i.e., the sympatho-adrenomedullary (SAM) axis and hypothalamic-pituitary-adrenal (HPA) axis, and the General Adaptation Syndrome (GAS).

Paragraph 2 AO2 *Evidence for*

Evidence for includes Selye's research and the fact that the 'fight or flight' response can be measured, e.g., pulse rate or sweating (using the galvanic skin response). Also, research into stress and illness supports the effects of stress on the body, e.g., Kiecolt-Glaser et al. (1984).

Paragraph 3 AO2 *Evidence against*

Evidence against includes the fact that they ignore psychological factors that are also involved, e.g., self-perception, see the definition of stress. Also, individual differences that modify the effects of stress show that it is not solely a physiological response, e.g., individual differences in self-perception, gender, personality, culture, and coping ability/self-efficacy. Research evidence is based on natural experiments and correlations, and so cause and effect cannot be inferred as the IV has not been controlled. Thus, whilst the effects of stress on the body are incontrovertible, conclusive findings are difficult as in real life more than two variables are involved in such a complex response; there are multiple causes and effects. Also include criticisms of the GAS, e.g., extrapolation from rats, and that it is not a non-specific response as we do not respond in the same way to all stressors, i.e., different stressors have different effects.

Conclusion AO2

The physiological response is indisputable but it only accounts for nature not nurture. It may be more representative of men than women as Taylor suggests that 'fight or flight' is valid for men, but women's stress response differs and has named this 'tend and befriend'. This is only one level of the stress experience that also occurs at a behavioural, cognitive, unconscious, and emotional level, and so it is reductionist (oversimplified) and incomprehensive to only consider the physiological responses to stress.

2. Consider the extent to which research (theories and/or studies) shows a relationship between stress and illness. (18 marks)

Paragraph 1 AO1

Define stress and explain how the hypothalamic-pituitary-adrenal axis (immunosuppression), sympatho-adrenomedullary axis (high blood pressure and glucose), and GAS (exhaustion) stages link to stress and illness.

Paragraph 2 AO2 *Evidence for*

Evidence for a relationship between stress and illness includes studies by Rahe et al. (1970), Kiecolt-Glaser et al. (1984; 1995), Friedman and Rosenman (1974), Cohen et al. (1991), and Ganster et al. (1991). Give criticisms of this research (both positive and negative). For example: Evidence for because it shows that... but... give negative criticisms.

Paragraph 3 AO2 *Evidence against*

A positive link between stress and illness ignores psychological factors and individual differences, i.e., self-perception, gender, personality, culture, and coping ability/self-efficacy. Research is correlational so not a causal relationship; other factors may be involved and so it lacks explanatory power. It is also based on self-report, which has problems of participant reactivity and response set. The research is biologically reductionist and deterministic. Whilst stress is associated with illness, stress at all of the different levels (cognitive, emotional, behavioural) must be accounted for.

Conclusion AO2

Weigh up and consider that a multi-perspective is needed to understand the multiple variables in the relationship between stress and illness.

3. Consider the extent to which research (theories and/or studies) shows a relationship between stress and cardiovascular disorders. (18 marks)

Same as answer to question 2 but leave out any reference to immunosuppression.

4. Consider the extent to which research (theories and/or studies) shows a relationship between stress and suppression of the immune system. (18 marks)

Same as answer to question 2 but leave out any reference to cardiovascular disorders.

5. Outline and evaluate research (theories and/or studies) into life changes as a source of stress. (18 marks)

Paragraph 1 AO1

Define life changes and outline the Social Readjustment Rating Scale (SRRS), i.e., 43 life events, and how these require adjustment and so absorb psychic energy.

Paragraph 2 AO2 *Evidence for*

Evidence for is the positive correlation found by Holmes and Rahe (1969), Rahe et al. (1970), and Rahe and Arthur (1977).

Paragraph 3 AO2 *Evidence against*

Evidence against is the criticisms of the SRRS and because correlations are weak, other factors may contribute to stress. The SRRS is biased by participant reactivity. The values are already attached to it and so it does not draw on participants' real experiences so may lack mundane realism and ecological validity. It is used widely, which testifies to its real-life validity. But it is suggested that daily hassles are a more likely source of stress. It ignores individual differences and psychological factors, which might explain why the correlations were weak. Also life events are not objective, but subjective, stressors that will be modified by individual differences in self-perception, personality (particularly the fact that some are more hardy than others), gender, and culture. A key weakness of the SRRS is that it does not account for self-perception. Thus, life changes do contribute to stress, but the measure has weaknesses and in real life more than just two variables are involved.

Conclusion AO2

It is impossible to quantify the contribution of life changes to stress as they are difficult to measure and cannot be isolated from the effects of other factors. Weigh up contributions/positive applications and weaknesses.

6. Outline and evaluate research (theories and/or studies) into the workplace as a source of stress. (18 marks)

Paragraph 1 AO1

Define workplace stressors and outline control and interpersonal relationships as sources of workplace stress and how this can lead to disaffection (duvet days), burnout, and mental illness.

Paragraph 2 AO2 *Evidence for*

Evidence Marmot et al. (1997) (control), includes studies by Glass et al. (1969), Brady (1958), Shirom (1989), and Margolis and Kroes (1974).

Paragraph 3 AO2 *Evidence against*

The relationship is correlational not causal hence other factors may be involved. These are not objective but subjective stressors that are modified by individual differences in self-perception, personality, gender, and culture. Also give methodological criticisms of the research both positive and negative (e.g., sample-bias, participant reactivity, researcher effects, reliability, and validity). Hence, evidence is limited and may lack validity, which means it lacks explanatory power as the findings may not be true and a lack of external validity means they lack generalisability to other populations. The individual differences limit generalisability.

Conclusion AO2

It is impossible to quantify the contribution of workplace stressors to the experience of stress as there are multiple causes and effects in this experience. Weigh up contributions vs. limitations.

7. To what extent do individual differences modify the effects of stress? (18 marks)

Paragraph 1 AO1

Outline the role of self-perception using the transactional model (see the definition of stress). Also identify personality and gender.

Paragraph 2 AO2 *Evidence for*

Evidence for individual differences modifying the effects of stress includes Type A/B, hardy personality, physiological (hormones), and psychological (socialisation), gender differences, and the effect of culture, e.g., acculturative stress and hypertension, and differences in social support between individualistic and collectivistic cultures. Also individual differences in self-perception and coping ability.

Paragraph 3 AO2 *Evidence against*

Evidence against individual differences modifying the effects of stress is that stress is biological; we all experience physiological reactivity (SAM, HPA, and GAS) hence there is not great variation. Also, are research findings on individual differences valid or do limitations mean explanatory power is limited (i.e., criticise the research evidence given in paragraph 2)? Is the stress response more similar than different (i.e., we all experience a similar physiological response)?

Conclusion AO2

Weigh up the evidence for and against.

8. Outline and evaluate the role of personality in stress. (18 marks)

Separate out just the bits on personality from question 7.

9. Outline and evaluate the role of gender in stress. (18 marks)

Separate out just the bits on gender from question 7.

10. Outline and evaluate the physiological approach to stress management. (18 marks)

See 'Example essay question on stress management'.

11. Outline and evaluate the psychological approach to stress management. (18 marks)

Paragraph 1 AO1

Define psychological approach to stress management and outline stress inoculation training (Meichenbaum: assessment, stress-reduction techniques, applications) and increasing hardiness (Kobasa: focusing, reconstruction, and compensation through self-improvement).

Paragraph 2 AO2

Evaluate these techniques in a positive way. They do address cognition and so may be treating the underlying causes, which will alleviate the symptoms. They also combine cognitive and behavioural principles, which is effective because more than one level is being targeted. They also increase control and self-efficacy, which may explain their effectiveness.

Paragraph 3 AO2

Now provide your criticism. These techniques do require self-insight; the patient must be able to assess/focus and they are time-consuming. The effects may not be felt for some time and so require perseverance and patience. They do not work for everybody and are not based on representative research, and so may have limited generalisability. There is a lack of hard evidence to support the methods. Most importantly, they ignore nature/biological factors. You should expand on this point.

Conclusion AO2

Weigh up the techniques.

Stress Crib Sheets

Cross-reference with Brody and Dwyer's revision guide, the stress APFCCs, findings/conclusions (in the Appendices), essay plans, and AO1 revision summary.

Definitions

Stress: ....
....

Stressor: ....
....

General Adaptation Syndrome (GAS): ....
....

Immune system: ....
....

Cardiovascular disorders: ....
....

Life changes: ....
....

Workplace stressor: ....
....

Stress management: ....
....

Physiological approaches to stress management: ....
....

Psychological approaches to stress management: ....
....

The body's response to stress

Sympatho-adrenomedullary (SAM) axis: The effect of the hypothalamus on the sympathetic branch of the ANS causes: ....
....
....

Hypothalamic-pituitary-adrenal (HPA) axis: The effect of the hypothalamus on the pituitary and adrenal glands causes: ....
....

The GAS: ....
....
....

Evaluation of the physiological response
Reductionist: ....

Ignores psychological factors (emotion, cognition, learning): ....
....

Ignores individual differences: ....
....

The relationship between stress and physical illness

The exhaustion stage of the GAS: ....
....

The immune system: ....
....

The cardiovascular system: ....
....

Evaluation of the relationship between stress and illness
Correlational not causal: ....
....

Ignores psychological factors: ....
....

Ignores individual differences: ....
....

Evidence is inconclusive: ....
....
....

Sources of stress

Life changes as measured by the SRRS: ....
....
....

AO2: ....
....
....

Workplace stressors, i.e., environmental aspects, control, and interpersonal relationships:
....
....

AO2: ....
....
....

Individual differences modify stress

Personality: Type A/B: ....
....

Hardy personality: ....
....

AO2: Cause and effect: ....
....

Self-report method: ....
....

Gender: Physiological differences in hormones: ....
....

Psychological differences in gender socialisation: ....
....

AO2: Differences as great within as between: ....
....

Nature/nurture: ....
....

Stress management

Physiological approaches: Anti-anxiety drugs: ....
....

AO2: ....
....
....

Biofeedback: ....
....

AO2: ....
....

Psychological approaches: Stress inoculation training (SIT): ....
....

AO2: ....
....

Hardiness training: ....
....

AO2: ....
....

Abnormality Learning Objectives

On completion of this topic you should be familiar with the following.

Defining psychological abnormality

- Define the term abnormality and know the definitions that are used to establish whether someone is abnormal: statistical infrequency, deviation from social norms, deviation from ideal mental health, and failure to function adequately.
- Describe and evaluate the definitions of abnormality, for example cultural relativism can be used to assess the definitions as culturally relative.

Biological and psychological models of abnormality

- Discuss the assumptions made on the causes of abnormality by the models of abnormality, i.e., explain what the causes are based upon (e.g., with the biological model, causes based upon abnormality being a mental illness with a physical basis).
- Evaluate the biological and psychological (including behavioural, psychodynamic, and cognitive) models of abnormality.

Critical issue—Eating disorders: Anorexia nervosa and bulimia nervosa

- Describe the clinical characteristics of anorexia nervosa and bulimia nervosa, distinguish between the two disorders, and be able to define eating disorders, anorexia nervosa, and bulimia nervosa.
- Assess the biological and psychological explanations of eating disorders.
- Describe the Aims, Procedures, Findings, Conclusions, and Criticisms (APFCCs) for a study of the biological explanations of eating disorders, for example, Holland et al.'s (1988) 'genetic vulnerability in anorexics' and a study into psychological explanations of eating disorders, for example Behar et al.'s (2001) 'the effect of gender identity on anorexics and bulimics'.

Cross-reference the above learning objectives with the Specification and fill in the self-assessment box below on completion of the topic.

SELF-ASSESSMENT BOX

☺ **Which of the above do you know?**

☹ **Are there any gaps in your knowledge that need to be targeted during revision?**

Defining Psychological Abnormality

For details, see Eysenck's textbook (page 183) and Brody and Dwyer's revision guide (page 90). Use the cues in the table to guide your note taking and fill in the gaps using the letter clues provided.

Definition of abnormality

Definition of statistical infrequency

Description

Statistically infrequent behaviour deviates from the mean of the n_____ d_____n. If the behaviour is r_____, i.e., shown by few people, then it is abnormal.

Ψ Give examples of statistically infrequent behaviour:

Evaluation

Ψ Desirability of infrequent behaviours.

Ψ The standard (statistical norm) is relative to the population that is being measured.

Definition of deviation from social norms

Description

Behaviour that deviates from the n_____ and v_____ of society, that is, the approved and expected ways of b_____g in a particular society, is considered to be abnormal. This is called socially d_____t behaviour and can be compared with non-conformity.

Ψ Give examples of behaviour that deviates from social norms:

Evaluation

Ψ Subjectivity and era-dependence of moral codes.

Ψ Culturally relative.

Definition of deviation from ideal mental health

Description

This is based on the h_____ approach and so the emphasis is on fulfilling one's potential, which is called s_____-a_____. Jahoda (1958) suggested six 'elements for optimal living':

1. S_____-a_____   4. A_____

2. P_____ g_____   5. P_____ of r_____

3. I_____   6. E_____ m_____

Evaluation

Ψ The focus on positive characteristics is good.

Ψ Culturally relative, as not all of the characteristics generalise to collectivist cultures, e.g., autonomy.

Definition of failure to function adequately

Description

Failure to function adequately refers to failure to fulfil in_____, s_____, and o_____ roles. Rosenhan and Seligman (1989) suggested seven features of abnormality:

1. S_____

2. M_____

3. V_____ and u_____ of behaviour

4. U_____ and l_____ of c_____

5. I_____ and i_____

6. O_____ d_____

7. V_____ of m_____ and i_____ s_____

Evaluation

Ψ Value judgements mean assessment is difficult and may be unreliable.

Ψ Culturally relative, as judgements will be influenced by cultural norms, e.g., unconventionality.

The multi-perspective approach to defining abnormality

The difficulty in defining abnormality has led to the conclusion that there is no precise distinction between abnormal and normal, and so a continuum is the best way to define abnormality. This is normally distributed with normal and abnormal at either end and most people fall somewhere in the middle.

NORMAL ⟵ *(Where do you fall on the continuum?)* ⟶ ABNORMAL

The key criticism of *all* definitions of abnormality is cultural relativism.

So what is cultural relativism?

Using this in the exam

AO1 questions:

Explain what is meant by the terms abnormality/statistical infrequency/deviation from social norms/deviation from ideal mental health/failure to function adequately. (3 + 3 marks or 2 + 2 + 2 marks)
Two or three of these terms may be specified, and marks allocated accordingly.

Outline two attempts to define abnormality. (3 + 3 marks)
Two definitions may be specified.

Outline the failure to function adequately definition of abnormality and give one criticism of this definition. (3 + 3 marks)

Give two criticisms of the statistical infrequency definition of abnormality. (3 + 3 marks)

Essay questions:

Consider how well definitions of abnormality account for cultural differences. (18 marks)
Outline and evaluate <u>two or more</u> definitions of abnormality. (18 marks)

Models of Abnormality

For details, see Eysenck's textbook (page 193) and Brody and Dwyer's revision guide (page 94). Fill in the gaps using the letter clues provided and use the cues in the table to guide your note taking.

Biological (medical) model

Description

This model uses p_____l i_____s as a model for psychological disorder. Thus, abnormality has physical c_____ such as b_____ dysfunction (neurological), biochemical imbalances, infection, or genetics, and so can only be cured through m_____. It is the dominant model as medical practitioners naturally favour it but it has been expanded upon by the d_____–stress model, which sees abnormality as an interaction of g_____ pre_____ and e_____.

Assumptions on the causes of abnormality

Ψ Infection.

Ψ Genetic factors.

Ψ Biochemistry.

Ψ Neuroanatomy.

Evaluation

Ψ Research evidence is based on well-established science.

Ψ The model has validity as it successfully explains phenylketonuria (PKU).

Ψ It does provide insights into schizophrenia and depression.

Ψ The analogy to physical illness is limited.

Ψ Cause and effect is not clear.

Ψ Does not give enough consideration to psychological and social factors and so is biologically deterministic and reductionist.

Ψ Anti-psychiatry, e.g. Szasz's 'problems in living'.

Ψ Ethical implications.

Using this in the exam

AO1 questions:

Outline two assumptions of the biological model in relation to the causes of abnormality.   (3 + 3 marks)
Outline implications of the biological model of abnormal behaviour.   (6 marks)
Give two criticisms of the biological model of abnormality.   (3 + 3 marks)

Psychodynamic model

Description

This model focuses on the dynamics of the mind. According to F_____, the mind is like an iceberg with the tip representing conscious thought, and the majority representing the preconscious and the u_____, which we are unaware of and cannot access. Material is r_____ into the un_____ if it is a source of c_____t. The unconscious develops during c_____ and is the key motivator of adult thinking and behaviour. Thus, conflicts during childhood that have not been re_____ are the cause of abnormality.

Assumptions on the causes of abnormality

Ψ Conflict between the id, ego, and superego.

Ψ Fixation at psychosexual stages due to conflict.

Ψ Defence mechanisms that help control conflict.

Evaluation

Ψ Positive implications of Freud's work— psychoanalysis paved the way for later psychological models.

Ψ Evidence does support childhood as a factor in the development of abnormality.

Ψ Does not give enough consideration to adult experiences and can be criticised as being deterministic.

Ψ Overemphasis on sexual factors and underemphasis on social factors.

Ψ Clinical interview was the main research method and so there is a lack of scientific evidence.

Ψ Concepts are vague and cannot be operationalised, and so cannot be verified or falsified.

Ψ Ethical implications.

Using this in the exam

AO1 questions:

Outline two assumptions of the psychodynamic model in relation to the causes of abnormality. (3 + 3 marks)

Outline implications of the psychodynamic model of abnormal behaviour. (6 marks)

Give two criticisms of the psychodynamic model of abnormality. (3 + 3 marks)

Behavioural model

Description

This model is based on the principles of l_____ and the assumption that all behaviour is learned through a_____ (c_____ conditioning), r_____ (o_____ conditioning), or social learning (s_____ l_____ t_____). Abnormality is a result of learning mal_____ and dysfunctional b_____.

Assumptions on the causes of abnormality	Evaluation
Ψ Classical conditioning (Pavlov, 1927).	Ψ Underlying causes are ignored because the behaviourists refuse to investigate internal processes. They investigate only that which is observable and measurable, i.e., behaviour, and so ignore the influence of cognition and emotion.
	Ψ Consequently therapies treat symptoms not causes.
Ψ Operant conditioning (Skinner, 1938).	Ψ The behavioural therapies do work well for phobias.
	Ψ Exaggerates the importance of environmental factors and so is environmentally deterministic.
	Ψ Extrapolation of Pavlov's and Skinner's research from animals must be questioned.
Ψ Social learning theory (Bandura, 1965).	Ψ Artificiality of lab research means ecological validity can be questioned.
	Ψ Oversimplified and so reductionist.
	Ψ Ethical implications.

Using this in the exam

AO1 questions:

Outline two assumptions of the behavioural model in relation to the causes of abnormality.   (3 + 3 marks)

Outline implications of the behavioural model of abnormal behaviour.   (6 marks)

Give two criticisms of the behavioural model of abnormality.   (3 + 3 marks)

Cognitive model

Description

This model suggests cognitive d_____ underpins abnormality. The individual is an inf_____ pro_____ and it is a breakdown in c_____ processing that causes abnormality. Irrational, obsessive, and faulty thinking can affect e_____ and b_____.

Assumptions on the causes of abnormality	Evaluation
Ψ Cognitive dysfunction.	Ψ The model has validity (i.e., truth) as it helps to explain anxiety disorders and depression.
	Ψ Cause and effect is not clear.
	Ψ The cognitive model has led to the development of the cognitive-behavioural model.
	Ψ Ignores other important factors such as genetics and social factors.
	Ψ Ethical implications.

Conclusion: The multi-dimensional approach

To fully understand ab_____ b_____ a multi-dimensional approach is necessary that draws from all of the m_____ of a_____. A particularly useful example is expressed by the diathesis–stress model that takes into account the interaction of g_____ pre_____ (diathesis) and en_____ (stress) to explain psychological disorder. Thus, according to the d_____–s_____ model, 'the g____ loads the gun but the e_____t pulls the trigger'.

Using this in the exam

AO1 questions:

Outline two assumptions of the cognitive model in relation to the causes of abnormality.   (3 + 3 marks)
Outline assumptions of the behavioural model on the treatment of abnormality.   (6 marks)
Give two criticisms of the cognitive model of abnormality.   (3 + 3 marks)

Essay questions:

Outline and evaluate two models of abnormality.   (18 marks)
This allows you to choose which two models you prefer to write about. Alternatively the question may specify ONE or TWO particular models or give you a choice between two, e.g.:
Outline and evaluate either the biological or behavioural model as a way of explaining abnormal behaviour.   (18 marks)
Outline and evaluate either the psychodynamic or cognitive model as a way of explaining abnormal behaviour.   (18 marks)
Outline key features of the <u>biological, behavioural, psychodynamic, cognitive</u> model of abnormality and consider its strengths and/or limitations. OR Give a brief account of the _____ model of abnormality and consider its strengths and limitations.   (18 marks)

Eating Disorders

For details, see Eysenck's textbook (page 208) and Brody and Dwyer's revision guide (page 202). Use the cues in the table to guide your note taking and fill in the gaps using the letter clues provided.

Definition of an eating disorder

Definition of anorexia nervosa

Clinical characteristics

Ψ W_____

Ψ Am_____

Ψ B_____ i_____ di_____

Ψ An_____

Ψ Age of onset tends to be during a_____e

Ψ Prevalence of the disorder in individuals with the following characteristics:

Definition of bulimia nervosa

Clinical characteristics

Ψ B_____

Ψ P_____

Ψ Fr_____

Ψ B_____ i_____

Ψ Age of onset tends to be during early a_____d

Ψ Prevalence of the disorder in individuals with the following characteristics:

Comparing and contrasting anorexia and bulimia

Traits that sufferers with each condition have in common

Ψ Distorted body image.

Ψ Obsessive thinking.

Ψ Dysfunctional eating behaviour.

Differences between anorexics and bulimics

Ψ Weight.

Ψ Eating patterns.

Ψ Age of onset.

Garner (1986) argues that there is an overlap between a_____ and b_____. The term 'anorexiabulimia' describes sufferers who show characteristics of both disorders, e.g., between 30–50% of anorexics b_____ and p_____, and bulimics may fast. Moreover, some sufferers move between the two d_____. However, some forms are entirely distinct, e.g., restrictive anorexia compared to obese bulimia. The diverse expression of anorexia and bulimia means that some cases are s_____ and others are d_____.

Using this in the exam

AO1 questions:

Explain what is meant by the terms eating disorder, anorexia nervosa, and bulimia nervosa.   (2 + 2 + 2 marks)

Outline the clinical characteristics of anorexia nervosa.   (6 marks)

Outline the clinical characteristics of bulimia nervosa.   (6 marks)

Outline three clinical characteristics of anorexia nervosa.   (2 + 2 + 2 marks)

Outline three clinical characteristics of bulimia nervosa.   (2 + 2 + 2 marks)

Outline two (or three) characteristics that are common to anorexia nervosa
and bulimia nervosa.   (3 + 3 marks or 2 + 2 + 2 marks)

Outline two or three differences in the characteristics of anorexia nervosa
and bulimia nervosa.   (3 + 3 marks or 2 + 2 + 2 marks)

This content could also be used as AO1 in an essay question on eating disorders, but remember to keep it limited as AO1 should form only one-third of the marks and you are likely to describe some of the explanations also; see the next worksheet on 'Explanations of eating disorders'.

Explanations of Eating Disorders

For details, see Eysenck's textbook (page 210) and Brody and Dwyer's revision guide (page 102). Use the cues in the table to guide your note taking and fill in the gaps using the letter clues provided.

> **EXAM TIP**: Many of the explanations relate to both anorexia and bulimia and so the explanations are covered as explanations of eating disorders to avoid repetition. In the exam you may be asked to describe or evaluate an explanation of eating disorders, or anorexia or bulimia may be specified. So note carefully if the following explanations apply to both disorders and note clearly if they are used to explain just anorexia or bulimia. You could also be asked an APFCC question on the explanations of eating disorders so please complete the abnormality APFCCs.

Biological explanations

Description

Ψ Genetic factors.

Ψ Biochemical factors.

Ψ Neuroanatomy.

Evaluation

Ψ Not 100% concordance rates and so other factors must be involved; genetics predispose rather than cause the conditions.

Ψ Cause, effect, or correlate?

Ψ Reductionist because it is oversimplistic to reduce complex behaviour to biological mechanisms only.

Ψ Ignores nurture, i.e., psychological and social factors.

Psychological explanations

Behavioural

Ψ Classical conditioning (Leitenberg et al., 1968).

Ψ Operant conditioning (Rosen & Leitenberg, 1985).

Ψ Social learning theory—modelling (Barlow & Durand, 1995; Nasser, 1986).

Ψ Culture-bound syndrome.

Evaluation

Ψ Behavioural explanations do not account for individual differences in vulnerability.

Ψ May explain maintenance more than cause.

Ψ Social learning theory accounts for cognition and appears to be valid (correct) as can account for a sudden increase.

Psychodynamic

Ψ Sexual development.

Ψ Family systems theory (Minuchin et al., 1978): conflict, overprotectiveness, rigidity, enmeshment (note the mnemonic CORE).

Ψ Autonomy and identity confusion (Bruch, 1971).

Evaluation

Ψ Conflict—cause or consequence?

Ψ Doesn't account for sudden increase in eating disorders.

Ψ Psychodynamic explanations are based on case studies and clinical interviews that lack objectivity and thus scientific validity.

Ψ Lack of scientific evidence means these explanations cannot be verified or falsified.

Cognitive

Ψ Distortion of body image (Garfinkel & Garner, 1982; Cooper & Taylor, 1988).

Ψ Cognitive dysfunction, e.g., obsessive thinking and perfectionism.

Evaluation

Ψ Research evidence is scientific as based on the experimental method.

Ψ Cognitive dysfunction—cause or consequence?

Conclusions

A m_____-d_____l approach is needed to fully account for eating disorders. The compromise position of the d_____–s_____ model best accounts for the influence of nature (g_____) and nurture (e_____) and so is the most comprehensive account of a_____ and/or b_____.

Using this in the exam

AO1 questions:

Outline the APFCC of one study into the biological explanations of <u>eating disorders.</u>	(6 marks)
Outline the APFCC of one study into the psychological explanations of <u>eating disorders.</u>	(6 marks)
Describe the findings (or conclusions) of research into the <u>biological/psychological</u> causes of <u>eating disorders</u>.	(6 marks)
Describe one <u>biological/psychological</u> explanation of <u>anorexia nervosa/bulimia nervosa/ eating disorders</u>.	(6 marks)
Outline two <u>biological/psychological</u> explanations of <u>anorexia nervosa/bulimia nervosa/ eating disorders</u>.	(3 + 3 marks)
Outline one <u>biological/psychological</u> explanation of <u>anorexia nervosa/bulimia nervosa/ eating disorders</u> and give one criticism of this explanation.	(3 + 3 marks)
Give two criticisms of a <u>biological/psychological</u> explanation of <u>anorexia nervosa/ bulimia nervosa/eating disorders</u>.	(3 + 3 marks)

Essay questions:

Consider whether psychologists have been successful in explaining anorexia nervosa <u>and/or</u> bulimia nervosa using a biological approach.	(18 marks)
Consider whether psychologists have been successful in explaining anorexia nervosa <u>and/or</u> bulimia nervosa using a psychological approach.	(18 marks)
With reference to one or more explanations, consider how successful psychologists have been in accounting for <u>anorexia nervosa/bulimia nervosa/eating disorders</u>.	(18 marks)
Outline and evaluate any two explanations of <u>anorexia nervosa/bulimia nervosa/eating disorders</u>.	(18 marks)
Consider whether research supports the view that eating disorders are caused by biological factors.	(18 marks)
Consider whether research supports the view that eating disorders are caused by psychological factors.	(18 marks)

EXAM TIP: Exam questions usually specify whether they require biological or psychological, anorexia or bulimia content. So where there is underlined text this is to show the various possibilities. You should prepare an answer for all of the possibilities rather than rely on being given a choice between anorexia and bulimia, or biological and psychological.

Abnormality APFCCs

EXAM TIP: You need to know a study demonstrating a biological and psychological explanation for both anorexia nervosa and bulimia nervosa; hence, the four APFCCs that follow. However, you could be asked for research findings (or conclusions) into anorexia or bulimia. Hence, you must be aware of more research findings or conclusions. Cross-reference with the completed APFCCs in the appendix of the Brody and Dwyer revision guide (pages 188–190).

A study into biological explanations of anorexia—Holland et al.'s (1988) study of genetic vulnerability in anorexics

Aims:

Procedures:

Findings:

Conclusions:

Criticisms:

A study into psychological explanations of anorexia and bulimia —Behar et al.'s (2001) study of the effect of gender identity on anorexics and bulimics

Aims:

Procedures:

Findings:

Conclusions:

Criticisms:

Abnormality Revision AO1

Use this as a checklist, i.e., tick off when you feel confident you can answer the following questions and/or have prepared a model answer for each type of question. The range of potential exam questions is finite so you can prepare for all possibilities.

Definition questions (2 + 2 + 2 marks or 3 + 3 marks)

You may be asked to define any of the terms that appear on the Specification, except for those that are given as examples. So, cross-reference with the Specification.

EXAM TIP: Give examples to make sure you get all of the marks!

Abnormality	Anorexia nervosa	Bulimia nervosa
Eating disorder	Statistical infrequency	Deviation from social norms
Deviation from ideal mental health	Failure to function adequately	

Definitions

Cross-reference with the glossary in the Brody and Dwyer revision guide (pages 193–202).

Example exam question: What is meant by the terms… *[and two or three of the following would be stated]*

Abnormality:

Anorexia nervosa:

Bulimia nervosa:

Eating disorder:

Statistical infrequency:

Deviation from social norms:

Deviation from ideal mental health:

Failure to function adequately:

Research questions (3 + 3 marks or 6 marks)

Cross-reference with the completed APFCCs in the appendix of the Brody and Dwyer revision guide (pages 188–190).

Example exam questions: Describe the aims/procedures/findings/conclusions/one criticism of a study into… *[any two aspects could be specified]* (6 marks)

Describe the findings of research into… (6 marks)

Describe the conclusions of research into… (6 marks)

Give two criticisms of research into… (3 + 3 marks)

EXAM TIP: Each part of the APFCC should be about 3 minutes' worth of writing. Hence, it should take you 6 minutes to answer the question, which is equivalent to the total number of marks.

Make sure you can give the APFCC for the following studies and further studies if findings/conclusions are asked for.

Q: Describe the APFCC of one study into the biological causes of eating disorders. OR findings/conclusions.

A: Holland et al. (1988) or Kendler et al. (1991), and both if findings/conclusions.

Q: Describe the APFCC of one study into the psychological causes of eating disorders. OR findings/conclusions.

A: Behar et al. (2001) or Jaeger et al. (2002), and both if findings/conclusions.

These studies are of course not the only answers that could be given but this does limit the number of studies that need to be remembered! However, you could be asked to give findings (or conclusions) only so do revise closely the other studies covered on the 'Explanations of eating disorders' worksheet.

Explanations/theories questions (6 marks or 3 + 3 marks)

These questions could be worded in a number of ways.

Example exam questions: Describe one explanation of… (6 marks)

Outline two explanations of… (3 + 3 marks)

Describe one explanation and give one criticism of… (3 + 3 marks)

Outline the main features of… (6 marks)

Outline two factors that explain… (3 + 3 marks)

Outline two factors that influence… (3 + 3 marks)

Outline two ways that… (3 + 3 marks)

Outline two effects of… (3 + 3 marks)

EXAM TIP: The definitions and content from the APFCCs are relevant to many of these questions.

Q: Describe the statistical infrequency/deviation from social norms/deviation from ideal mental health/failure to function adequately definition *[any could be specified]*. OR Outline two definitions of abnormality. OR Outline one definition of abnormality and give one criticism of it.

A: See definitions of deviation from statistical, social norms, ideal mental health, and failure to function adequately in 'Defining psychological abnormality'.

Q: Outline two factors that influence definitions of abnormality.

A: Cultural relativism and era-dependence, and use examples to illustrate. See 'Defining psychological abnormality'.

Q: Outline two assumptions of the biological/behavioural/cognitive/psychodynamic model *[any could be specified]* in relation to the causes of abnormality.

A: Describe two causes of the biological (genes, biochemical imbalance), behavioural (classically conditioned associations, reinforcement), cognitive (cognitive dysfunction, breakdown in information processing), or psychodynamic (unconscious conflicts, regression) model as appropriate to the question. See 'Models of abnormality'.

Q: Describe one assumption of the biological/behavioural/cognitive/psychodynamic model *[any could be specified]* in relation to the causes of abnormality and give one criticism of this model.

A: Describe one cause of the biological, behavioural, cognitive, or psychodynamic model as appropriate to the question and give one criticism. See 'Models of abnormality'.

Q: Describe one biological explanation of anorexia nervosa/bulimia nervosa/eating disorders *[any could be specified]*. OR Outline two... OR Outline one and give one criticism.

A: Genetic predisposition and hypothalamus dysfunction. See 'Explanations of eating disorders' and the APFCC and later criticisms.

Q: Describe one psychological explanation of anorexia nervosa/bulimia nervosa/eating disorders *[any could be specified]*. OR Outline two... OR Outline one and give one criticism.

A: Modelling as suggested by social learning theory and as illustrated by the APFCC on psychological explanations and faulty cognitions. See 'Explanations of eating disorders' and later criticisms.

Q: Outline two factors that explain anorexia nervosa/bulimia nervosa or eating disorders.

A: Either the biological or psychological explanations identified above could be used.

Q: Describe the clinical characteristics of anorexia nervosa or bulimia nervosa.

A: Describe three in enough detail for 2 marks each. For example: Anorexia: weight, amenorrhoea, body image distortion, anxiety, age of onset. Bulimia: binge–purging, frequency, body image, age of onset. See 'Eating disorders'.

> **EXAM TIP**: Behavioural, cognitive, and psychodynamic are not specified on the Specification under explanations of eating disorders, therefore exam questions will be on *psychological* explanations.

Comparison questions (2 + 2 + 2 marks or 3 + 3 marks)

Example exam question: Give two or three differences between...

(3 + 3 marks or 2 + 2 + 2 marks)

> **EXAM TIP**: You are more likely to be asked about differences than you are about similarities.

Q: Describe two or three differences/similarities in the characteristics of anorexia nervosa and bulimia nervosa.

A: For example, weight, eating patterns, and age of onset. See 'Eating disorders'.

Criticism questions (3 + 3 marks or 6 marks)

Example exam questions: Give two criticisms of... (3 + 3 marks)
Outline one explanation and give one criticism... (3 + 3 marks)

Remember you need to know two criticisms for each of the above explanations/theories and the APFCCs.

Q: Give two criticisms of the statistical infrequency/deviation from social norms/deviation from ideal mental health/failure to function adequately definition *[any one could be specified]*.

A: Remember most of the definitions rely on value judgements and are culturally relative. See 'Defining psychological abnormality'.

EXAM TIP: You must be able to evaluate the different approaches to abnormality, e.g., biological versus psychological. The criticisms of the models and the explanations of eating disorders do overlap, which should help your recall. Here are some generic criticisms that can be applied to any model/explanation:

Q: Give two criticisms of the biological model of abnormality/explanations of eating disorders *[either one could be specified]*.

A: Reductionist: an attempt to explain a complex phenomena by focusing on one less complex component of the whole and ignores other levels of explanation, and nurture; and biologically deterministic: ignores the influence of the individual (or free will as the humanists argue) on their own behaviour.

Q: Give two criticisms of the behavioural/psychodynamic/cognitive model of abnormality/explanations of eating disorders *[either one could be specified]*.

A: Reductionism applies to all of the models and environmental, developmental, and cognitive determinism apply to the behavioural, psychodynamic, and cognitive model explanations respectively. Also, nature is ignored.

Example Essay Question on Eating Disorders

With reference to one or more explanations, consider how successful psychologists have been in accounting for anorexia nervosa. (18 marks)

Paragraph 1: AO1—Define anorexia nervosa and identify different explanations

Anorexia nervosa is an eating disorder characterised by the individual being severely underweight: 85% or less than expected for size and height; anxiety/fear of becoming fat; and a distorted body image. The individual does not have an accurate perception of their own, or 'normal', body size. Many biological and psychological explanations have been proposed. Biological explanations include genetics, infection, brain dysfunction, and biochemical imbalances; psychological explanations include behavioural, which explain anorexia in terms of maladaptive learning through conditioning and modelling theory; psychodynamic, which link anorexia to sexual development and family conflict; and cognitive, which explain anorexia in terms of faulty information processing.

Paragraph 2: AO2—Evaluate the biological explanations

Ψ Genetics (twin studies)

The genetic explanation is reductionist (oversimplified) because it just considers the influence of biology and ignores the role of nurture. Certainly nurture plays a role, as the concordance rate found by Holland et al. in their study of genetic vulnerability in anorexics was 56% and there are no 100% concordance rates for anorexia. Thus, factors other than genetics must be involved. However, the high percentage may well be indicative of a strong genetic basis, which means this explanation does have validity.

Ψ Hypothalamus dysfunction

The 'stop/start' mechanism of the VMH and LH is also a reductionist explanation as it ignores key psychological factors that must be important as anorexics do feel hungry and so it is not simply the case that their 'start' switch is damaged; rather their cognitions override this switch. Thus, the biological explanations of anorexia lack conviction and do not provide a complete explanation of eating disorders as they ignore psychological factors such as cognition, emotion, and motivation.

Paragraph 3: AO2—Evaluate the psychological explanations

Ψ Classical and operant conditioning

The behavioural explanations based on conditioning theory are reductionist as they also only focus on one component (learning). Furthermore, the biological and behavioural explanations are limited because they explain anorexia in terms of the pathological individual, when eating disorders must be linked to cultural norms given that they are considered to be a Western culture-bound syndrome.

Ψ Social learning theory

Modelling theory based on social learning theory offers a less reductionist explanation as it accounts for anorexia as a cultural phenomenon, i.e., that anorexia is a social construction and a product of the norms and values of Western society. That is, it is a 'sick society' rather than a 'sick individual'. Thus, this explanation has real-life validity, but it does not explain why some are more affected by the idealised images than others, or why the disorder persists once the 'ideal' body size has been achieved. Thus, individual factors must be considered to account for such variation, e.g., faulty cognitions, the effect of the disorder on physiology, reinforcement history, and so on.

Conclusion: AO2

Psychologists have successfully identified many levels of explanation that account for anorexia. Psychologists taking just one perspective would not be able to account for anorexia as this would be reductionist; no single explanation can account for disorder. However, many psychologists take a multi-perspective as proposed by the diathesis–stress model, which is the most convincing and useful account of disorder to date—'the genes load the gun, but it is the environment that pulls the trigger'. Psychologists who do take into account the interaction of individual and cultural causative factors are best able to account for eating disorders.

Abnormality Essay Plans

1. Outline and evaluate two definitions of abnormality. (18 marks)

Paragraph 1 AO1

Identify two definitions. Deviation from ideal mental health (Jahoda, 6 criteria: self-attitudes, personal growth, integration, autonomy, perception of reality, environmental mastery) and failure to function adequately (7 abnormal characteristics: suffering, maladaptiveness, vividness and unconventionality, irrationality and unpredictability, incomprehensibility, observer discomfort, and violation of moral and ideal standards) will provide the most AO1.

Paragraph 2 AO2

Cultural relativism: Assess the cultural relativism of autonomy as it is an individualistic not a collectivistic ideal. Also assess the cultural relativism of interpretations of behaviour, i.e., what would be considered bizarre, irrational, environmental mastery, incomprehensible, or a violation of moral and ideal standards depends on culturally constructed norms. Use examples to support this, e.g., sexuality, drugs, social customs, and rituals.

Paragraph 3 AO2

Era-dependence: Do the same as above but this time use examples to show how constructions change over time, e.g., homosexuality.

Conclusion

Consider how universality contradicts cultural relativism and so weigh up the extent to which the definitions do have generalisability.

2. Consider how well definitions of abnormality account for cultural differences. (18 marks)

Paragraph 1 AO1

Identify the definitions of abnormality and define cultural relativism.

Paragraph 2 AO2 *Evidence for*

Consider the impact of culture on social norms, ideal mental health criteria, and failure to function adequately characteristics. These defintions are culturally biased as they are based upon individualistic culture, e.g., ideal mental health. Cross-cultural differences in conceptions of abnormality are evident in attitudes to sexuality and drugs. Also cross-cultural differences in diagnosis, expression of symptoms, and the existence of culture-bound syndromes all support the fact that abnormality is defined differently across cultures.

Paragraph 3 AO2 *Evidence against*

Universality of abnormal disorder. Abnormality exists in all cultures but is just labelled differently. Abnormality has biological causes, which leaves little room for culturally different social constructions.

Conclusion AO2

Weigh up the evidence for and against.

3. Outline and evaluate two models of abnormality. (18 marks)

Paragraph 1 AO1/AO2

Outline causes of the biological model (genetics, biochemicals, and neuroanatomy) and evaluate. See the crib sheets for ideas. Use research evidence to support and contradict. Most importantly, the biological model ignores nurture and the psychological causes of abnormality, e.g., internal factors (the psyche and unconscious conflicts) as covered by the psychodynamic model, cognitive (faulty thinking), and external factors (the environment) as covered by the behavioural model and so is reductionist (oversimplified) and it is biologically deterministic because it ignores the free will of the individual to control their own behaviour.

Paragraph 2 AO1/AO2

Outline causes of the behavioural model (classical and operant conditioning, and social learning theory) and evaluate. See the crib sheets for ideas. Use research evidence to support and contradict. Consider reductionism and determinism.

Paragraph 3 AO2

Consider that no single model accounts for abnormality, it exists at a number of levels and so the main criticism of both models is that they are reductionist; they only account for one factor, biological (biology), or behavioural (environment). Considering the different levels abnormality exists at, a multi-perspective is needed to account for it. Nature and nurture must be accounted for, but the biological and behavioural explanations only account for one or the other. Use the alternative models (i.e., psychodynamic and cognitive) as further criticism.

Conclusion AO2

The models need to take a compromise position, as the diathesis–stress model does, i.e., a multi-perspective needs to be taken.

4. Outline and evaluate two explanations of eating disorders. (18 marks)

Use the above plan to help with this as there is a lot of overlap.

Paragraph 1 AO1

Outline and evaluate the biological explanations (gene, hypothalamus dysfunction, biochemicals). Use research evidence, so see the APFCCs and the crib sheets. For example, Holland et al. (1988), Garfinkel and Garner (1982), Kendler et al. (1991), and Fava et al. (1989). Positive evaluation is the scientific support for these explanations. But they are reductionist and deterministic, ignore nurture and psychological factors, and cause and effect is not clear as evidence is correlational or natural experiments. For example, the biochemical imbalances identified by Fava et al. (1989) may be a cause of anorexia, an effect, or a correlate.

Paragraph 2 AO2

Outline and evaluate the behavioural explanations (classical conditioning and weight phobias, operant conditioning, positive reinforcement, i.e., compliments, and negative reinforcement, i.e., avoid feeling unhappy about weight, and modelling theory). Use research evidence so see the APFCCs and the crib sheets. For example, Behar et al. (2001), Jaegar et al. (2002), Barlow and Durand (1995), and Lee et al. (1992).

Paragraph 3 AO2

Multi-perspective is needed as both explanations are reductionist. Even in combination they ignore the cognitions and unconscious conflicts identified by alternative explanations.

Conclusion AO2

The models need to take a compromise position, as the diathesis–stress model does, i.e., a multi-perspective needs to be taken.

5. Consider whether research supports the view that eating disorders are caused by biological factors. (18 marks)

Paragraph 1 AO1

Outline biological explanations of the causes of anorexia/bulimia. See above.

Paragraph 2 AO2

Research evidence for includes Holland et al. (1988), Kendler et al. (1991), Garfinkel and Garner (1982), and Fava et al. (1989).

Paragraph 3 AO2

Evidence against is that they ignore psychological factors and so do not account for nurture. They are reductionist and deterministic and most importantly do not account for eating disorders as a cultural phenomenon. They explain eating disorders as an individual pathology rather than putting the blame on society. Use research evidence that supports the psychological factors and so contradicts the biological, e.g., Behar et al.

Conclusion AO2

Multi-perspective and diathesis–stress model.

6. Consider whether research supports the view that eating disorders are caused by psychological factors.

(18 marks)

Paragraph 1 AO1

Outline psychological explanations of the causes of anorexia/bulimia, i.e., learning explanations: conditioning (classical and operant) and modelling (social learning theory); psychodynamic: sexual development, enmeshment and identity confusion; and cognitive: faulty thinking, e.g., body image and perfectionism.

Paragraph 2 AO2

Evidence for is Behar et al. (2001), Minuchin et al. (1978), and Bruch (1971). Give positive and negative criticisms of this research. You could consider the real-life explanatory power of social learning theory as it accounts for eating disorders as a cultural phenomenon, which Behar et al. (2001) and Jaegar et al. (2002) support.

Paragraph 3 AO3

Evidence against is that they ignore biological causes/nature. Use research evidence in support of the biological causes, which contradicts psychological explanations.

Conclusion AO2

Multi-perspective and diathesis–stress model.

7. With reference to one or more explanations, consider how successful psychologists have been in accounting for eating disorders.

(18 marks)

See 'Example essay question on eating disorders'.

Abnormality Crib Sheets

Cross-reference with Brody and Dwyer's revision guide, the abnormality APFCCs, findings/conclusions (in the Appendices), essay plans, and AO1 revision summary.

Definitions

Abnormality: ....
....

Statistical infrequency: ....
....

Deviation from social norms: ....
....

Deviation from ideal mental health: ....
....

Failure to function adequately: ....
....

Eating disorder: ....
....

Anorexia nervosa: ....
....

Bulimia nervosa: ....
....

Definitions of abnormality

Statistical infrequency: ....
....

AO2: ....
Deviation from social norms: ....
....

AO2: ....
Deviation from ideal mental health: ....
....

AO2: ....
Failure to function adequately: ....
....

AO2: ....
Cultural relativism: ....
....

Era-dependence: ....
....

Models of abnormality—causes

Biological (medical) model—genetic factors: ....
....

Biochemistry: ....

Neuroanatomy: ....

AO2: Ignores nurture: ....

Cause or correlate: ....

Scientific support: ....

Reductionist and deterministic: ....
....

Psychodynamic model: Unconscious conflicts: ....
....

Stages of psychosexual development: ....
....

Defence mechanisms: ....
....

AO2: Introduced psychological factors to the concept of mental illness: ....
....

Relevance to today's society where there are fewer taboos: ....
....

Non-scientific: ....

Overemphasis on past ignores current problems: ....

Overemphasis on sex ignores social causes: ....

Behavioural model—classical conditioning: ....
....

Operant conditioning: ....
....

Social learning theory: ....
....

AO2: Ignores nature: ....
....

Focus on symptoms not causes: ....
....

Does account for influence of culture: ....
....

Cognitive model—faulty information processing: ....
....

The cognitive triad: ....
....

AO2: Responsibility can be positive and negative: ....
....

Reductionist as ignores other causes: ....
....

Clinical characteristics

Anorexia nervosa: ....

Bulimia nervosa: ....

Differences between the two:

1. ....

2. ....

3. ....

Explanations of eating disorders

Biological explanations—biological causes—nature

Genetic factors: ....

Biochemical: ....

Neuroanatomy: ....

AO2: Not 100% concordance: ....

Cause, effect, or correlate: ....

Reductionist as ignores other factors: ....

Behavioural explanations—maladaptive learning—nurture

Classical and operant conditioning: ....

Social learning theory—modelling and culture-bound syndrome: ....

AO2: Explains maintenance more than causes: ....

Deterministic: ....

Reductionist as ignores other factors: ....

Social learning theory does account for society: ....

Psychodynamic explanations—early childhood conflicts

Sexual development: ....

Enmeshed family: ....

Autonomy and identity confusion: ....

AO2: Family conflict may be a consequence: ....

Overemphasis on past, not enough on present: ....

Unfalsifiable and unverifiable: ....

Cognitive explanations—faulty information processing, cognitive dysfunction

Body image distortion and perfectionism: ....

AO2: Cause or effect: ....

Social Influence Learning Objectives

On completion of this topic you should be familiar with the following.

Majority and minority influence

- Define majority influence (conformity) and minority influence.
- Distinguish between majority and minority influence.
- Describe the Aims, Procedures, Findings, Conclusions, and Criticisms (APFCC) for a study of majority influence, e.g., Asch's (1951) 'line study' and a study of minority influence, e.g., Moscovici et al.'s (1969) 'calling a blue slide green'.
- Outline two explanations of majority influence, informational influence, and normative influence (Deutsch & Gerard, 1955).
- Describe the three kinds of conformity: compliance, identification, and internalisation (Kelman, 1958).
- Outline two explanations of minority influence, e.g., Moscovici's (1985) four conditions for conversion and Latané and Wolf's (1981) social impact theory.

Obedience

- Define obedience to authority and distinguish between this and majority influence.
- Describe the APFCC for a study of obedience, e.g., Milgram's (1963) 'electric shock experiment'.
- Assess the internal validity and external validity of the above study and be able to define these terms.
- Outline two explanations of obedience, e.g., agentic shift and the authoritarian personality.
- Describe explanations of resistance to obedience, e.g., reduce the influence of the experimenter and increase the obviousness of the learner's distress.

Critical issue—Ethical issues in psychological research

- Define the terms ethical guidelines, ethical issues, deception, informed consent, and protection of the participants from psychological harm.
- Describe the ethical issues raised by social influence research, in particular deception, informed consent, and protection of participants from psychological harm.
- Distinguish between ethical issues and ethical guidelines.
- Discuss how these issues are dealt with, e.g., ethical guidelines, ethical committees, and cost–benefit analyses.

Cross-reference the above learning objectives with the Specification and fill in the self-assessment box below on completion of the topic.

SELF-ASSESSMENT BOX

☺ **Which of the above do you know?**

☹ **Are there any gaps in your knowledge that need to be targeted during revision?**

Majority Influence

For details, see Eysenck's textbook (page 227) and Brody and Dwyer's revision guide (page 111). Fill in the gaps using the letter clues provided and use the cues in the table to guide your note taking.

Majority influence or c_____ is a form of s_____ i_____ where we want to be liked by other people and so in part it is our desire to b_____g or fit in. Consequently, we experience gr_____ pr_____ to conform to the n_____ of the majority.

You could also be asked an APFCC question on this so please complete the majority influence APFCC.

Definition of majority influence (conformity)

Explanations of conformity (Deutsch & Gerard, 1955)	
N_____e influence	I_____l influence

Types of conformity (Kelman, 1958)		
Compliance	**Identification**	**Internalisation**
Ψ Change your b_____ but not your m_____.	Ψ Change your b_____ to fit in with the g_____.	Ψ Change your m_____ and b_____.

Factors that influence conformity	
Culture (Smith & Bond, 1993)	**Historical context (Perrin & Spencer, 1980)**
Ψ Individualistic vs. collectivistic cultures.	Ψ The Asch effect was a 'c_____ of its t____'.

Using this in the exam

AO1 questions:

Explain what is meant by the terms majority influence and minority influence.	(3 + 3 marks)
Describe the APFCC of one study that has explored majority influence.	(6 marks)
Describe the findings/conclusions of one study that has explored majority influence.	(6 marks)
Describe two explanations of why people yield to majority influence.	(3 + 3 marks)
Outline two psychological processes involved in conformity to majority influence.	(3 + 3 marks)
Outline two factors that influence majority influence.	(3 + 3 marks)

Minority Influence

For details, see Eysenck's textbook (page 233) and Brody and Dwyer's revision guide (page 116). Fill in the gaps using the letter clues provided and use the cues in the table to guide your note taking.

G_____p p_____e can be resisted as this is what occurs when people yield to m_____ i_____ as first they must have rejected the majority norm. The many real-life examples of minority influence show its potential to bring about reform. The process by which the minority influences the ma_____ is called c_____n. People often c_____ with the majority whilst p_____y they are c_____ the position of the minority.

You may be asked an APFCC question so please complete the APFCC on minority influence.

Definition of minority influence

Explanations of minority influence	
Conditions for conversion (Moscovici, 1985) Ψ Consistency. Ψ Flexibility. Ψ Commitment. Ψ Relevance.	**Social impact theory (Latané & Wolf, 1981) is a general explanation of social influence that also explains majority influence** Ψ Strength. Ψ Status and knowledge. Ψ Immediacy.

Differences between majority and minority influence	
Majority influence Ψ Compliance. Ψ Takes place immediately. Ψ High need for approval.	**Minority influence** Ψ Conversion. Ψ Takes place over time. Ψ Lower need for approval.

Using this in the exam

AO1 questions:

Explain what is meant by the terms minority influence and social influence.	(3 + 3 marks)
Describe the APFCC of one study that has explored minority influence.	(6 marks)
Describe the findings/conclusions of one study that has explored minority influence.	(6 marks)
Outline two explanations of why people yield to minority influence.	(3 + 3 marks)
Outline two psychological processes involved in (or explanations of) minority influence.	(3 + 3 marks)
Outline two (or three) differences between majority and minority influence.	(3 + 3 marks or 2 + 2 + 2 marks)

Obedience

For details, see Eysenck's textbook (page 243) and Brody and Dwyer's revision guide (page 120). Use the cues in the table to guide your note taking.

Obedience is when we do what we are told. Is this on the decline? Discuss.

You may also be asked an APFCC question on this so please complete the obedience APFCC.

Definition of obedience to authority

Explanations of obedience	
Agentic state—a situational factor	Authoritarian personality—a personal factor

Differences between obedience and conformity	
Obedience	**Conformity**
Ψ Social influence is based on hierarchy.	Ψ Social influence is based on equal status.
Ψ Explicit.	Ψ Implicit.
Ψ Participants embrace obedience as an explanation of their behaviour.	Ψ Participants deny conformity as an explanation of their behaviour.

Methodological Criticisms of Milgram's Research

For details, see Eysenck's textbook (page 247) and Brody and Dwyer's revision guide (page 122?). Use the cues in the table to guide your note taking.

Orne and Holland (1968) have criticised the validity of Milgram's research. What is meant by the term 'validity'? There are two types of validity (see below).

Definition of internal validity

Definition of external validity

Example task

Your task is to draw a line to match up the following statements with the correct term that appears on the right-hand side. More than one term may apply. Identify whether the research in the statement HAS or LACKS the term you match it to. For example:

The experimental design did the job it set out to do. ◄—— HAS ——► **Internal validity**

The participants couldn't have believed in the set-up.   **Mundane realism**

The study can be applied to other settings.

Obedience is a demand characteristic.   **Internal validity**
Artificial laboratory research may not be
representative of real life.

The participants showed signs of real distress.   **Experimental realism**

An experiment is a social situation and so a
reflection of life.

Milgram's research has been successfully replicated in   **External validity**
more natural situations.

Ψ So what does this mean in terms of validity and realism?

Internal validity

Evidence for experimental realism

Ψ Evidence provided by Milgram, e.g., video tapes.

Ψ Participants' reactions.

Evidence against experimental realism

Ψ Demand characteristics.

External validity

Evidence for external validity

Ψ Milgram's variation in a run-down office.

Ψ Cross-cultural replications.

Ψ Further studies, e.g., Hofling et al. (1966) and Bickman (1974).

Ψ Generalisability to the Nazi atrocities of the Holocaust.

Evidence against external validity

Ψ Lacks mundane realism.

Ψ Limited generalisability to current setting.

Ψ The external validity of the further studies can be questioned.

Conclusions

There are persuasive arg_____ for and against the v_____ of Milgram's research. His research has many w_____. However, the findings are still important as the research participants' belief that they were delivering el_____ shocks supports e_____ r_____m and so i_____ v_____y. Furthermore, the findings illustrated the fundamental attribution error, which is the tendency to u_____ the role of s_____ factors and o_____ the role of p_____ factors. Milgram's conclusion that the situational context was highly influential has been applied to the atrocities of the H_____, which demonstrates the gen_____ and thus e_____l v_____y of the research.

Resistance to Obedience

For details, see Eysenck's textbook (page 246) and Brody and Dwyer's revision guide (page 124). Use the cues in the table to guide your note taking.

Milgram (1974) carried out many variations of his original remote-victim experiment. Two factors increased resistance to obedience. In the box below, write down the obedience percentages for each variation to see how much obedience reduced and resistance increased. Also, write down some details about the different variations. What is your comparison percentage (i.e., Milgram's original finding)?

Reducing the influence of the experimenter
Ψ Location of the experiment = ___ %
Ψ Orders by telephone = ____ %
Ψ A disobedient role-model = ___ %
Increasing the obviousness of the learner's distress
Ψ Voice feedback = ___ %
Ψ Proximity—1 metre away = ___ %
Ψ Touch-proximity—hand on shockplate = ___ %

Using this in the exam

AO1 questions:

Explain what is meant by the terms obedience to authority, internal validity, and external validity. (2 + 2 + 2 marks)

Explain what is meant by the term external validity and illustrate your answer with reference to one study of obedience to authority. (3 + 3 marks)

Describe the APFCC of one study that has investigated obedience to authority. (6 marks)

Describe the findings/conclusions of one study that has investigated obedience to authority. (6 marks)

Outline two psychological processes that may be involved in obedience to authority. (3 + 3 marks)

Outline two factors that influence obedience to authority. (3 + 3 marks)

Explain two ways in which people might resist obedience to authority. (3 + 3 marks)

Essay questions:

Consider the extent to which findings from obedience research be applied beyond the research setting. (18 marks)
Or you could be asked the same question about social influence research, so you could use obedience, majority influence, and minority influence.

Consider the extent to which the validity of obedience research be defended against criticisms. (18 marks)

Consider the extent to which social influence research displays <u>internal/external validity</u>. (18 marks)

Ethical Guidelines and Issues

For details, see Eysenck's textbook (page 261) and Brody and Dwyer's revision guide (page 127). Use the cues in the table to guide your note taking.

	Ethical issues	Ethical guidelines
Deception		
Informed consent		
Protection of participants from psychological harm		
Confidentiality		
Debrief		
Right to withdraw		

Ethical issues arose during the implementing of social influence research. Ethical guidelines have consequently been introduced to set standards for the conduct of research. The guidelines did not exist at the time of the research and so they were only broken retrospectively.

Ethical Debate

Asch's (1951, 1956) study of majority influence (conformity) in an unambiguous situation	
For: yes, the ends justify the means Ψ Methodological justifications— validity/importance of the findings. Ψ Participants' comments on their participation. Ψ Were ethical issues resolved?	**Against: no, the ends do not justify the means** Ψ Ethical issues. Ψ Critics of the research. Ψ Ethical issues that remained unresolved.

Zimbardo's (1973) study of conformity to social roles	
For: yes, the ends justify the means Ψ Methodological justifications— validity/importance of the findings. Ψ Participants' comments on their experience. Ψ Were ethical issues resolved?	**Against: no, the ends do not justify the means** Ψ Ethical issues. Ψ Critics of the research. Ψ Ethical issues that remained unresolved.

Milgram's (1963) study of obedience to authority

For: yes, the ends justify the means	Against: no, the ends do not justify the means
Ψ Methodological justifications—validity/importance of the findings.	Ψ Ethical issues.
Ψ Participants' comments on their experience.	Ψ Critics of the research.
Ψ Were ethical issues resolved?	Ψ Ethical issues that remained unresolved.

Conclusions

The research may be justified on m_____l grounds if a study is considered to have validity and so its findings make a s_____l c_____n, and on e_____l grounds if it is decided that the e_____ justify the m_____. The methodological criticisms question the validity and so value of the research and so reduce the likelihood that the ends justify the means. This is assessed at the outset through a c_____–b_____ analysis, which tries to ensure that the d_____n is ethical rather than moral. However, as the decision often lies with the individual researcher then the analysis is open to b____. Furthermore, qu_____ the costs and benefits may be difficult and it is not always possible to predict the o_____e (costs/benefits) of research at the o_____t, as Milgram's research illustrates.

Using this in the exam

AO1 questions:

Outline two ethical issues that have arisen in social influence research. (3 + 3 marks)
You must explain the issues in the research, not just ethical issues in general.
Describe how psychologists deal with the ethical issues that arise in psychological research. (6 marks)

Essay questions:

From your knowledge of the ethical issues involved in social influence research, to what extent can such research be justified? (18 marks)
Assess whether psychologists have been successful in resolving the ethical issues raised by social influence research. OR Outline and evaluate how psychologists have dealt with ethical issues (e.g., the use of ethical guidelines). (18 marks)
Consider the extent to which the importance of social influence research justifies the methods used in its investigation. (18 marks)
Consider the extent to which it is appropriate to judge social influence research carried out by psychologists (e.g., Asch, Milgram) as unethical. (18 marks)
Briefly outline some of the procedures used in social influence/majority influence/minority influence/obedience research and evaluate whether such procedures are ethical. (18 marks)

Resolving Ethical Issues

Definition of ethical issues

Definition of ethical guidelines

Effectiveness of ethical guidelines and ethical committees

Ψ How well does the debrief resolve ethical issues?

Ψ Do the guidelines set clear standards?

Ψ Impose limitations with some success, e.g., Charter status.

Ψ Lack legislative power.

Ψ Penalties for infringement lack censure.

Ψ No universal ethical truths as guidelines differ across cultures.

Ψ Managerial rather than a social ethic.

Ψ Interpretations of the guidelines and decisions by the committees are subject to bias and value judgements.

When considering whether the ends justify the means, a cost–benefit analysis needs to be done.

Cost–benefit analysis

The double-obligation dilemma
Ψ Means: costs to participants.

Ψ Ends: benefits to society.

Evaluation
Ψ Difficult to predict outcomes.

Ψ Quantification is difficult.

Ψ Researcher bias and value judgements.

Ψ Decision is a moral dilemma, which is what the guidelines aimed to stop.

Conclusions

The ethical g_____, committees, and c_____–b_____ analysis lack l_____ power because the s_____ they set are not statutory requirements. Thus, the safeguards put in place to resolve e_____ i_____ have limited effectiveness. The responsibility for good conduct lies with the individual researcher, which means that breaches do occur, where the rights of p_____ are sacrificed for the good of s_____ or d_____ is considered justifiable on methodological grounds, i.e., to avoid d_____ c_____. It is questionable whether the ends do justify the means in such cases and so further safeguards are necessary such as an external statutory regulatory body to control *what* research takes place, and *whether* it should take place.

Social Influence APFCCs

Study of obedience—Milgram's (1963, 1974) electric shock experiment

Aims:

Procedures:

Findings:

Conclusions:

Criticisms:

Study of majority influence (conformity)—Asch's (1951) line study
Aims:
Procedures:
Findings:
Conclusions:
Criticisms:

Study of minority influence—Moscovici et al.'s (1969) calling a blue slide green
Aims:
Procedures:
Findings:
Conclusions:
Criticisms:

Social Influence Revision AO1

Use this as a checklist, i.e., tick off when you feel confident you can answer the following questions and/or have prepared a model answer for each type of question. The range of potential exam questions is finite so you can prepare for all possibilities.

Definition questions (2 + 2 + 2 marks or 3 + 3 marks)

You may be asked to define any of the terms that appear on the Specification, except for those that are given as examples. So cross-reference with the Specification.

EXAM TIP: Remember to give examples to make sure you get all of the marks.

Social influence	Majority influence	Minority influence
Obedience to authority	Internal validity	External validity
Ethical guidelines	Ethical issues	Deception
Informed consent	Protection of participants from psychological harm	

Definitions

Cross-reference with the glossary in the Brody and Dwyer revision guide (pages 193–202).

Example exam question: What is meant by the terms... *[and two or three of the following would be stated]*

Social influence:

Majority influence:

Minority influence:

Obedience to authority:

Internal validity:
External validity:
Ethical guidelines:
Ethical issues:
Deception:
Informed consent:
Protection of participants from psychological harm:

Research questions (3 + 3 marks or 6 marks)

Cross-reference with the completed APFCCs in the appendix of the Brody and Dwyer revision guide (pages 190–192).

Example exam questions: Describe the aims/procedures/findings/conclusions/one criticism of a study into... *[any two aspects could be specified]* (6 marks)
Describe the findings of research into... (6 marks)
Describe the conclusions of research into... (6 marks)
Give two criticisms of research into... (3 + 3 marks)

> **EXAM TIP**: The question may ask for any two of the APFCCs or may just ask for the findings, conclusions, or two criticisms. So be prepared to give enough detail for 6 marks on the findings or conclusions and know two criticisms for all studies in sufficient detail for 3 marks each.

Make sure you can give the APFCC for the following social influence studies:

Q: Describe the APFCC of one study of majority influence. OR findings/conclusions.
A: Asch's (1951) 'line study', and Zimbardo (1973) if findings/conclusions.

Q: Describe the APFCC of one study of minority influence. OR findings/conclusions.
A: Moscovici et al.'s (1969) 'calling a blue slide green', and Nemeth et al. (1974) if findings/conclusions.

Q: Describe the APFCC of one study of obedience. OR findings/conclusions.
A: Milgram's (1963, 1974) 'remote victim' experiment, and the variations on this study if findings/conclusions.

Explanations/theories questions (3 + 3 marks or 6 marks)

These questions could be worded in a number of ways.

Example exam questions: Describe one explanation of... (6 marks)
Outline two explanations of... (3 + 3 marks)
Describe one explanation and give one criticism of... (3 + 3 marks)
Outline the main features of... (6 marks)
Outline two factors that explain reasons why people yield to... (3 + 3 marks)
Outline two factors that influence... (3 + 3 marks)
Outline two ways that... (3 + 3 marks)
Outline two effects of... (3 + 3 marks)

Q: Outline two psychological processes involved in majority influence (conformity).
A: Normative and informational influence. See 'Majority influence'.

Q: Outline two factors that influence conformity.
A: Cultural factors (Smith & Bond, 1993) and the historical context (Perrin & Spencer, 1980), and use research to illustrate. See 'Majority influence'.

Q: Identify and outline the three types of conformity.
A: Compliance, identification, and internalisation. See 'Majority influence'.

Q: Outline two explanations of minority influence. OR Outline two factors that explain minority influence.
A: Moscovici's four conditions for conversion, and social impact theory. See 'Minority influence'.

Q: Outline two psychological processes involved in obedience. OR Outline two factors that influence obedience.
A: Agentic state (a situational factor) and authoritarian personality (a personality factor); see 'Obedience'.

Q: Outline two explanations of resistance to obedience. OR Outline two factors that influence resistance to obedience.

A: Decreasing the responsibility of the experimenter, increasing the responsibility of the participant, and increasing the obviousness of the learner's distress. See 'Resistance to obedience'.

Q: Outline three ethical guidelines.

A: Deception, informed consent, and protection of participants from psychological harm. See definitions and 'Ethical guidelines and issues'.

Q: Outline two ethical issues in social influence research.

A: Focus on the issues not the guidelines. See 'Ethical guidelines and issues'.

Q: Outline two ways that psychologists deal with ethical issues.

A: The guidelines and cost–benefit analysis. See 'Ethical guidelines and issues' and 'Resolving ethical issues'.

Comparison questions (2 + 2 + 2 marks or 3 + 3 marks)

Example exam question: Give two or three differences between... (3 + 3 marks or 2 + 2 + 2 marks)

> **EXAM TIP**: Make sure you draw the comparison rather than describing each separately and expecting the examiner to identify the comparison as this would receive no marks!

Q: Describe three differences between conformity and obedience.

A: Hierarchy vs. equal status, explicit vs. implicit, embrace as an explanation of behaviour vs. reject as an explanation of behaviour. See 'Obedience'.

Q: Describe three differences between majority and minority influence.

A: Compliance vs. conversion, immediacy vs. takes place slowly, high need for approval vs. low need for approval. See 'Minority influence'.

Criticism questions (3 + 3 marks or 6 marks)

Example exam questions: Give two criticisms of... (3 + 3 marks)
Outline one explanation and give one criticism of... (3 + 3 marks)

Be prepared to criticise any of the APFCCs, and know two criticisms worth 3 marks each, as criticism questions are likely to be based on the research rather than the explanations/theories.

> **EXAM TIP**: Make sure you fully explain your criticism and relate it to the research to achieve all of the marks. Criticisms that apply to most of the studies include ethical and methodological:
>
> Ψ Ethical—identify the ethical issues. Q. Do the ends justify the means? See 'Ethical debate'.
> Ψ Methodological—mundane realism and ecological validity; or experimental realism and experimental validity. See 'Methodological criticisms of Milgram's research'.
> Ψ Insights provided and thus the social contribution of the research... A positive criticism!

Example Essay Question on Ethics

Consider the extent to which the use of deception can be justified in social influence studies.

(18 marks)

Paragraph 1: AO1

Ψ **Show you understand the question—Define deception, identify studies that have employed this, and outline the methodological reasons for deception**

Deception occurs when the participants are deceived as to the true nature and purpose of the research. There are methodological justifications for deception as complete openness could itself be a source of social influence as participant reactivity may occur. For example, in Asch's (1956) study of conformity and Milgram's (1963) study of obedience the research settings would lack experimental realism if deception had not been involved as participants aware of the research hypothesis may conform to the demand characteristics. Thus, rather than showing obedience or conformity the findings would show compliance (or reactance) to the demand characteristics and so the findings would lack experimental (internal) validity.

Ψ **AO2**

Thus, deception enables the tests of conformity and obedience to be valid, which provides strong methodological grounds for the use of deception in social influence studies.

Paragraph 2: AO2—Evidence for, i.e., the arguments that support deception

Ψ **Ethical justifications**

There are ethical justifications for the social influence studies. In his own defence, Milgram emphasised the role of the debriefing. This revealed the deception, provided reassurance to limit the emotional consequences, and included a survey where 84% said they were glad to have taken part and that there should be more research like this. Milgram claimed that the fact that the participants believed the research was acceptable and worthwhile did justify the means (deception) involved. Asch's participants admired the elegance of his design, which further demonstrates that participants can find deception acceptable. Furthermore, the deception did not cause permanent psychological harm as psychiatric reports of Milgram's participants one year later found no signs of long-term damage, which provides further justification for the use of deception.

Paragraph 3: AO2—Evidence against, i.e., the arguments that challenge deception

Ψ **Ethical criticisms**

Whilst there are ethical justifications there are also ethical criticisms. Baumrind (1964) is highly critical of the deception in Milgram's research. She claimed that Milgram violated the basic rights of his participants by deceiving them as to the true nature and purpose of the experiment. Social influence research is potentially damaging because participants are finding out about themselves as people, which may have emotional consequences. For example, Milgram's participants' self-esteem may have been affected by their destructive obedience. If the distress caused gives rise to permanent psychological damage then this casts doubt as to whether the deception was ethically justifiable.

Conclusion: AO2

Ψ **Do the ends justify the means? Cost–benefit analysis**

A cost–benefit analysis involves weighing up if the ends (benefits to society) justify the means (potential distress to participants). The results of social influence studies have contributed enormously to our understanding of human behaviour. Milgram's research has been described as 'morally significant' and 'a momentous and meaningful contribution' (Erikson, 1968). Thus, it could be argued that the benefits to society outweigh the distress to the participants. To conclude, deception can be defensible, but this should only be decided based upon careful cost–benefit analysis during which alternative procedures where deception is not used must be explored.

Social Influence Essay Plans

1. From your knowledge of the ethical issues involved in social influence research, to what extent can such research be justified? (18 marks)

   OR Consider the extent to which the importance of social influence research justifies the methods used in its investigation. (18 marks)

   OR Consider whether the findings from social influence research (e.g., Asch, Milgram, Zimbardo) can justify the methods used to obtain such findings. (18 marks)

   OR Consider the extent to which it is appropriate to judge social influence research carried out by psychologists (e.g., Asch, Milgram) as unethical. (18 marks)

   OR Briefly outline some of the procedures used in social influence research and evaluate whether such procedures are ethical. (18 marks)

Paragraph 1 AO1

Define and describe the ethical issues (e.g., deception, informed consent, right to withdraw, protection of participants from psychological harm) that arose in social influence research. You will probabaly choose to draw primarily from Milgram (1963), Asch (1951, 1956), and Zimbardo (1973) but you do not need to restrict yourself to these studies as there are many more you could refer to. DO NOT write a Milgram essay as the question is on social influence, not Milgram. Explain that in order to decide if research is justified a cost–benefit analysis should be conducted, which involves weighing up whether the ends justify the means and that this helps the researcher address the 'double-obligation dilemma' of the participants versus society.

Paragraph 2 AO2 *Evidence for*

Evidence that the ends did justify the means in social influence research is its contribution to society. For example, the greater understanding it gave us of majority influence, obedience, and minority influence. Furthermore, the research does have positive applications. For example, Zimbardo's research was used to improve prison systems and procedures. Furthermore, the social influence researchers have defended their work through claims that the means were actually acceptable to the participants and so the research is justifiable. For example, Asch claimed his participants admired the elegance of his design and Milgram stated that 84% of his participants were glad to have taken part and felt there should be more research like it. They have also defended their research against criticism that there was a lack of protection of participants. Milgram and Zimbardo have argued that the distress lasted only as long as the research and that, as there was no permanent harm, the ends did justify the means. Both claim that the debrief effectively resolved the issue of lack of protection as participants were given access to psychiatrists and Milgram followed this up with psychiatric assessment one year later, which found no signs of long-term damage. Furthermore, Milgram has claimed that it wasn't the means people had the real issue with, it was his findings.

Paragraph 3 AO2 *Evidence against*

Milgram's and Zimbardo's justifications/defence are of course highly subjective and not everybody accepts these. Baumrind (1964) and Savin (1973) argue that both Milgram's (1963) and Zimbardo's (1973) research is ethically unjustifiable because the studies violated the basic rights of the participants by deceiving them as to the true nature and purpose of the experiment and failed to protect them from psychological harm. Social influence research is potentially damaging because participants are finding out about themselves as people, which may have emotional consequences. For example, Milgram's participants' self-esteem may have been affected by their destructive obedience and, similarly, the guards in Zimbardo's research may have been distressed by their sadistic behaviour once out of the research environment. If the distress gave rise to permanent psychological damage then this casts doubt as to whether the social influence research was ethically justifiable.

Conclusion AO2

Milgram was investigated and cleared by the APA. A replication of Zimbardo's prison experiment has recently been passed by the BPS although the researchers behind 'The Experiment' claim that there are more stringent safegurds in their research. Conclude that each study must be considered individually through a cost–benefit analysis and weigh up whether you think the ends did justify the means.

2. Consider the extent to which Milgram's research helps us to understand why people obey. (18 marks)

Paragraph 1 AO1

Define obedience and identify the focus of Milgram's explanations, i.e., the influence of the situation.

The 'fundamental attribution error' and the situational explanation

Milgram's research has contributed significantly to our understanding of obedience as his rejection of the 'Germans are different' hypothesis radically changed post-Second World War views on destructive obedience. Prior to his findings, the accepted view was that obedience is a consequence of personality and that destructive obedience indicates a deviant personality, such as Adorno et al.'s (1950) authoritarian personality. Thus, Milgram's research illustrates the 'fundamental attribution error', i.e., overemphasis on personal factors and underemphasis on situational factors, and so does provide a better understanding of why people obey.

Paragraph 2 AO2 *Evidence for*

Evidence for the 'fundamental attribution error' and situational factors as an explanation of obedience is Milgram's agency theory, which considers agentic shift of responsibility as an explanation. Milgram's research also demonstrated the role of buffers, proximity, the research context, the role of disobedient role models, socialisation, and the binding factors/graduated commitment. Don't describe these in detail, instead use them as evidence to support the argument that Milgram has contributed to our understanding of obedience.

Significant contribution

Milgram himself claims the criticisms of his research were so strident more because of the significance of his findings than the weaknesses of his methodology. His research 'opened our eyes'...

Paragraph 3 AO2 *Evidence against*
Methodological criticisms

Orne and Holland (1968) question the internal and external validity of Milgram's research. Thus, his findings may lack truth and meaningfulness, which means his insights into obedience may be limited. Provide Orne and Holland's (1968) arguments that demand characteristics limit internal validity and mundane realism and that the institutional context and the time and context of the research limit external validity.

Conclusion AO2

Give Milgram's defence, e.g., film evidence and the debriefing Milgram claimed showed that the participants were genuinely deceived. Milgram's replication in a run-down office supports external validity. Also, he has generalised the insights into why people obey to the atrocities of the Second World War. Weigh up whether this is valid as there is both evidence for, e.g., obedience is higher if the victims are blamed, the psychological processes may be fundamentally similar, and against, e.g., the participants in Milgram's research needed to be watched and obedience dropped when the experimenter was not in the room. Also, disobedient peers decreased levels of obedience in Milgram's research but not in Nazi Germany, and Milgram's participants showed great distress whereas the Nazis showed little concern for personal or moral issues.

3. Consider the extent to which the findings from obedience research can be applied beyond the research setting. (18 marks)

Paragraph 1 AO1

Explain that the external validity of Milgram's research, i.e., generalisability beyond the research setting, was questioned by Orne and Holland (1968) because of the lack of mundane realism and the power of the institutional context. Elaborate on this, i.e., explain why there is a lack of mundane realism and what effect the institutional context has, e.g., the prestige and status of Yale University.

Paragraph 2 AO2 *Evidence for*

Evidence to support external validity is Milgram's variation in a run-down office building where 48% obedience was found rather that the 65% of the original study. Why does this support external validity?

Smith and Bond (1993) provide cross-cultural support for external validity as their findings were consistent with Milgram's in many other cultures. This is perhaps the strongest evidence that obedience research can be applied beyond the research setting as it suggests that the pressure and processes involved in obedience are more culturally universal than culturally relative. External validity is further supported by attempts to replicate the research, e.g., Hofling et al. (1966) and Bickman (1974). Don't describe the research in detail, just give the findings and conclusions that support external validity. Milgram's (1963) research has been replicated more successfully than Hofling et al.'s (1966) research, which supports generalisability beyond the research setting. Also consider whether the explanations of obedience revealed in the research are generalisable to the atrocities of the Second World War. See the plan for question 2 for more content on this.

Paragraph 3 AO2 *Evidence against*

All research is a product of the time and context in which it was produced, i.e., it is era-dependent and context-bound. Changes in society cause social constructions to change and this includes how we view authority figures. Contemporary society is more egalitarian, and status and authority have to be earned rather than ascribed. This change in attitudes to authority figures is supported by the replication of Zimbardo's research, 'The Experiment', where the guards were blatantly disrespected in spite of their position as authority figures. The status of the experimenter was significant in the original obedience research because when Milgram reduced this in later variations obedience did drop, as demonstrated by the drop in percentage of obedience in the run-down office variation. Given that the status of authority figures is different today, the temporal validity can be questioned. The research may not be generalisable from the research setting to the current context. You can also question whether the findings were generalisable at the time, as if you accept that the research lacked internal validity and mundane realism then you can conclude that the research is not representative of real-life obedience and so cannot be applied beyond the research setting. You could use the comparison of obedience research with Nazism to support this as many argue that the parallels are few and that Milgram's research does not explain the latter.

Conclusion AO2

Weigh up to what extent the findings from obedience research can be applied beyond the research setting, bearing in mind that Milgram's insights into obedience are still recognised and considered useful today.

4. Consider the extent to which the validity of obedience research can be defended. (18 marks)
   OR Consider whether criticisms of the validity of obedience research are justified. (18 marks)

Paragraph 1 AO1

Define internal and external validity and explain why these have been used by Orne and Holland (1968) to criticise obedience research.

Paragraph 2 AO2 *Evidence for*

To defend the validity, give Milgram's defence that his research had internal and external validity. Use the cross-cultural replications and later studies of obedience to support external validity. Consider that, whilst later studies such as Hofling et al.'s (1966) and Bickman's (1974) may seem to have greater mundane realism and so external validity, it is Milgram's that has faired better on replications, which is the true criteria for external validity. Discuss whether the research does generalise, i.e., have external validity, to the Nazi atrocities.

Paragraph 3 AO2 *Evidence against*

Question the defence, i.e., explain why it lacked validity. Evidence that the research does in fact lack validity lies in the methodological criticisms of internal (e.g., demand characteristics, sample bias, and so population validity) and external (e.g., mundane realism, reductionism, and artificiality) validity.

Conclusion AO2

Weigh up the criticisms against the defence. Consider that even though the research is artificial, the psychological processes of obedience may be the same in the research as in real life, in which case it has truth and real-life validity as it is applicable to real-life obedience. But does it? Ask yourself to what extent the research is era-dependent and context-bound and so lacks temporal validity. Use the plans for the questions above to help you plan this answer.

5. Outline some criticisms of majority influence research and consider whether these are fair. (18 marks)

Paragraph 1 AO1

Describe the methodological (e.g., sample bias, internal and external validity) and ethical (e.g., deception, informed consent, right to withdraw, protection of participants from psychological harm) issues that arose in majority influence research. You will probably choose to draw primarily from Asch (1951, 1956) and Zimbardo (1973) but you do not need to restrict yourself to these two studies as you could also include Jenness (1932), Sherif (1935), and Crutchfield (1954). DO NOT write about Milgram (i.e., obedience) or the minority influence research.

Paragraph 2 AO2 *Methodological criticisms—evidence for and against*

Assess whether methodological criticisms are justified. Both Asch and Zimbardo used only male (androcentric) samples and so population validity can be questioned as the findings may not be true of female participants. The samples also consisted only of students, which means generalisability to wider populations is low. This is a fair criticism because findings are not necessarily the same for both genders and their research displays a common gender bias, i.e., investigate men and use this as the standard for all human behaviour! The internal validity of Asch's research can be questioned as the research set-up may have revealed demand characteristics and hence the participants were conforming to experimenter expectancy rather than yielding to group pressure. However, the criticism can be questioned because the discomfort of the participants during the procedure testifies to their genuine deception and some reported afterwards that they were impressed by the elegance of the procedure, which suggests that they had been 'taken in'. The external validity of Asch's and Zimbardo's research can be questioned as both took place in an artificial environment. Asch's, in particular, lacked mundane realism as the task was trivial and so it is questionable whether the research is representative of conformity in real life. However, this criticism can be negated to some extent because in Zimbardo's research the participants did seem to experience the set-up as a real-life prison, demonstrated by the fact that one participant asked for parole. Asch's research has been replicated, which supports its external validity; the findings do seem generalisable and so the external validity criticism does not seem completely fair. Temporal validity is questioned as, according to Perrin and Spencer (1980), the Asch effect was 'a child of its time', as levels of conformity have decreased due to changing social constructions such as a greater emphasis on individuality. Smith and Bond's (1993) meta-analysis of studies that had used the Asch paradigm in the US supports this and so this criticism seems fair.

Paragraph 3 AO2 *Ethical criticisms—evidence for and against*

Assess whether ethical criticisms are justified. Deception/informed consent is a criticism mainly of Asch, but to a lesser extent of Zimbardo who hadn't revealed to the prisoner participants that they initially would be arrested at home. However, there are justifications for the way the research was conducted, e.g., Asch would not have obtained meaningful results unless deception had been used as demand characteristics would have reduced internal validity, and Zimbardo was trying to make the prisoners' experiences as real as possible. Both can also be criticised for a lack of protection of participants; Asch's experienced embarrassment and Zimbardo's suffered severely to the extent that some experiencing depression had to be withdrawn. Consider whether the debrief resolved the lack of protection issue. These are valid criticisms but it can be difficult, if not impossible, to meet the highest ethical standards as this interferes with the practicalities of research. Thus, it is necessary to conduct a cost–benefit analysis, which involves asking: do the ends justify the means? This leads to the 'double-obligation dilemma' of the participants versus society. Thus, it could be concluded that Asch's participants only suffered a little embarrassment during the research, which would not have continued afterwards and so the importance of the findings to society justified the temporary distress experienced. The dilemma is greater for Zimbardo's research because of the greater suffering of the participants. Thus, whilst ethical criticisms are valid, this does not mean that the research should not have taken place as many believe that, despite the criticisms, the ends did justify the means in majority influence research.

Conclusion AO2

Weigh up to what extent the methodological criticisms are fair by deciding if they greatly reduce the meaningfulness of the research and consider whether the ends justify the means.

6. Assess whether psychologists have been successful in resolving the ethical issues raised by social influence research.
OR Outline and evaluate how psychologists have dealt with ethical issues (e.g., the use of ethical guidelines). (18 marks)

Paragraph 1 AO1

Define ethical issues and identify what has been done to resolve these, e.g., the BPS ethical guidelines, ethics committees, the cost–benefit analysis, and charter status.

Paragraph 2 AO2 *Evidence for*

To show that they have been successful: The ethical guidelines do impose limitations and do constrain practising psychologists in particular because the charter status accorded by the BPS facilitates practice. Thus, the guidelines are upheld by the BPS and do have some sanctioning power in that charter status can be removed if the BPS code of conduct is violated. The guidelines do provide explicit guidance that supports psychologists in the management of research, i.e., they give guidance on 'how' to do the research. The debrief guideline is used to resolve issues that arise when other guidelines are not observed. Assess whether this is effective. Consider the strengths of ethical committees; they take the decision out of the hands of the individual who is more likely to be biased and so can make the decision more objective and fair. The cost–benefit analysis requires the researcher to stop and think about the consequences of the research and so ensures that serious thought is given to the possible research outcomes. This is a strength as it ensures, to some extent, that there is sufficient consideration within the research process.

Paragraph 3 AO2 *Evidence against*

To show that they have not been successful: However, the ethical guidelines lack censure as they have no legislative power and so are not enforceable partly because detection is also an issue. Because they differ across cultures, there are no universal ethical truths, and this reduces their authority. The ethical guidelines also lack sanctioning power because, whilst rogue psychologists found guilty of breaching the BPS code of conduct can be expelled from the BPS this does not stop them from continuing private practice. Furthermore, transgressions can be justified and so it is too easy to disregard the guidelines. The cost–benefit analysis also fails to fully resolve ethical issues because it is not always possible to predict outcomes, as Milgram's research illustrates by the fact that in his pilot study it was predicted that only complete psychopaths would go up to 450 volts but in fact 65% of the sample did! Also, it can be very difficult to quantify the cost and the benefits. Moreover, susceptibility of the analysis to researcher-bias is high and this is not necessarily removed at committee level. The ethical committes have a little more power in real life as the individual would have to find another institution to support their research if it was rejected by the committee. However, the committees could be biased, particulary if the research was likely to bring financial and/or status rewards. The over-commercialism of psychology is a current issue that supports the criticism that there are not enough safeguards and so the ethical committees are not a completely successful solution. In fact, the BPS is currently campaigning for an external statutory regulatory body that would be backed by the government. This suggests that they recognise the limitations of the present initiatives to resolve ethical issues. External assessment is common practice in teaching and medicine and would increase the objectivity of the cost–benefit analysis, and it could enable greater powers of censure to stop psychologists practising altogether if they violate the guidelines.

Conclusion AO2

Weigh up/assess the extent to which they have been successful/unsuccessful.

Social Influence Crib Sheets

Cross-reference with Brody and Dwyer's revision guide, the social influence APFCCs, finding/conclusions (in the Appendices), essay plans, and AO1 revision summary.

Definitions
Social influence: ....
Majority influence: ....
Minority influence: ....
Obedience to authority: ....
Internal validity: ....
External validity: ....
Ethical guidelines: ....
Ethical issues: ....
Protection of participants from psychological harm: ....
Deception: ....
Informed consent: ....
Comparison questions
3 differences between conformity and obedience: ....
3 differences between majority and minority influence: ....

Explanations of majority influence

Normative influence: Compliance and identification: ....
....
....
....

Informational influence: Internalisation: ....
....
....
....

Explanations of minority influence

4 conditions for conversion: ....
....
....
....

Social impact theory: ....
....
....
....

Explanations of obedience

Agentic state: ....
....
....
....

Authoritarian personality: ....
....
....
....

Explanations of resistance

Decrease authority of the experimenter and so increase responsibility of the participant: ....
....
....
....

Increase the obviousness of the learner's distress: ....
....
....
....

Methodological criticisms—relate these to the research

Experimental realism and internal validity: ....
....
....

Mundane realism and external validity: ....
....
....

Positive criticism of the social contribution of the research: ....
....
....

APFCC (see revision APFCCs)

Findings on majority influence: ....
....
....

Findings on minority influence: ....
....
....

Findings on obedience: ....
....
....

Ethical criticisms: Identify the issues raised by the research NOT the guidelines

Deception: ....
....
....

Informed consent: ....
....
....

Protection of participants: ....
....
....

Attempts to deal with ethical issues

Ethical guidelines: A code of conduct issued by the BPS and upheld by ethical committees:...
....

Cost–benefit analysis: A weighing-up of whether the ends justify the means: ....
....
....

Research Methods
Learning Objectives

On completion of this topic you should be familiar with the following things.

Describe and evaluate quantitative and qualitative methods
- *Experiments*: laboratory, field, quasi, and natural experiments.
- *Correlational analysis*: the interpretation of correlation coefficients, i.e., direction (positive and negative) and strength 0 = no correlation to 1 = perfect correlation.
- *Naturalistic observations*: overt and covert; participant and non-participant.
- *Questionnaires*: open-ended vs. closed questions.
- *Interviews*: structured vs. unstructured interviews.

Demonstrate competence in the design and implementation of research
- *Aims and hypotheses*: experimental (alternative), correlational, and other non-experimental hypotheses vs. the null hypothesis; directional vs. non-directional hypotheses.
- *Variables*: IV and DV (experimental), and V1 and V2 (correlational).
- *Experiment and research design*: independent measures (an experimental and control group; weakness participant variables), repeated measures (an experimental and control condition; weakness order effects), matched participants, and non-experimental research designs (e.g., naturalistic observation, interview, and questionnaire).
- *Factors associated with research design*: operationalisation of variables, pilot studies, confounding variables (e.g., participant (subject) variables and situational variables) and bias (e.g., investigator and participant effects), and how to control for these (e.g., random allocation, single/double-blind procedures, standardisation, counterbalancing).
- *Samples and populations*: types of sampling (e.g., opportunity and random); the issue of generalisability.
- *Reliability and validity*: how to test for and improve reliability and validity.

Analyse and describe quantitative data (descriptive statistics)
- *Levels of measurement*: nominal, ordinal, interval, ratio.
- *Measures of central tendency*: mode, median, mean.
- *Measures of dispersion*: range and standard deviation.
- *Graphs*: normal distribution, histogram, bar chart, frequency polygon, scattergram.

Analyse qualitative data
- *Content analysis*: making qualitative data quantitative through coding data into categories, also known as transcribing the data.
- *Discourse analysis*: analysis of words for patterns and themes.

Understand the following issues
- *Quantitative vs. qualitative methods*: advantages and weaknesses, which can be overcome to some extent by using a combined approach (called triangulation).
- *The scientific nature of psychology*: objectivity vs. subjectivity.
- *Ethical issues*: ethical issues that apply to psychological research.

Cross-reference the above learning objectives with the Specification and fill in the self-assessment box below on completion of the topic.

SELF-ASSESSMENT BOX

☺ **Which of the above do you know?**

☹ **Are there any gaps in your knowledge that need to be targeted during revision?**

Research Methods

For details, see Eysenck's textbook (pages 275) and Brody and Dwyer's revision guide (page 133). Fill in the gaps using the letter clues provided and use the cues to guide your note taking.

Research is the crux of psychology. In order to move beyond amateur and anecdotal explanations for behaviour we need research evidence to support the explanations or theories.

Research methods take either a qu_____ or qu_____ approach, which depends on whether the data collected is numerical or non-numerical. Thus, quantitative = n_____ and qualitative = w____. Quantitative methods are concerned with objective m_____ and so try to quantify and describe b_____r. In contrast, qualitative methods are concerned with gaining in-d___h data and so try to establish valid (true) ex_____ for behaviour. All methods can be used in a scientific or non-scientific way, so do not make the mistake of seeing quantitative as the former and qualitative as the latter. Both approaches have strengths and weaknesses and so should be seen as equally valuable. It is optimal to combine the approaches and this is called tr_____n.

Advantages and disadvantages
Give two advantages and two disadvantages for each of the following methods.

Laboratory experiments

The laboratory experiment takes place in a controlled environment and enables the experimenter to test the effect of the IV (independent variable) on the DV (dependent variable). In order to establish a difference and so detect cause and effect relationships, the IV is systematically varied between two conditions.

Field experiments

Field experiments take place in natural settings, e.g., a work environment. The experimenter has control of the IV and so causal relationships can be established.

Quasi-experiments

Quasi-experiments exist when the experimenter cannot control the IV; it is said to be naturally occurring. For example, experiments involving gender, age, class, or cultural differences would all be classed as quasi-experiments because the experimenter cannot manipulate any of these as the IV. However, the experimenter does have control of the research setting.

Natural experiments

A natural experiment is a kind of quasi-experiment, but the researcher has no control over the IV or the research setting.

Correlational analysis

Correlational analysis is a technique that measures the strength of the relationship between two variables. The paired scores of the two variables are analysed to establish the strength and direction of the association, e.g., the relationship between stress and illness. This can be illustrated visually through scattergrams and numerically through correlation coefficients. These range from +1 to 0 to −1, where the sign shows the direction, and the number shows the strength of the association.

Naturalistic observation

Naturalistic observation involves examining behaviour in a natural setting with minimal intrusion from the researcher as it aims to observe people's natural behaviour. Participants may be aware they are being observed (overt observation), or not (covert observation).

Interviews

Interviews can take many different forms: non-directive, informal, guided, clinical, or structured. They usually take place face-to-face and can yield rich, in-depth data.

Questionnaires

Written questionnaires are a type of interview. They can be conducted face-to-face, via the telephone, or by post. They consist of a standard set of questions that are either closed (fixed-response, e.g., rating scales) or open-ended (which allow detailed responses). Questionnaires are used to survey attitudes, beliefs, and behaviour.

Using this in the exam

The above exercise will prepare you for exam questions that ask you to select a suitable method or give the advantages and disadvantages of a particular method.

Identify the research method used in this investigation and explain one advantage and one disadvantage of this method. (1 + 2 + 2 marks)

Explain how you would implement (carry out) a... *[any of the methods could be identified].* (3 marks)

Aims and Hypotheses

For details, see Eysenck's textbook (page 296) and Brody and Dwyer's revision guide (page 145). Fill in the gaps using the letter clues provided and use the cues in the table to guide your note taking.

Aim: A general statement of why the study is being carried out
For example:
1. To investigate the effect of alcohol on perceived attractiveness of the opposite sex.
2. To investigate if women self-disclose more than men in a survey.
3. To investigate a gender difference in aggression.
4. To investigate the association between personality and self-esteem.
5. To investigate if chimps' behaviour does evidence a theory of mind.
6. To investigate the relationship between stress and illness.
See if you can decide whether the above aims would be tested as experimental, correlational, or non-experimental hypotheses. (Clue: there are two of each!)
Note the hypothesis number in the appropriate box below.

Hypothesis: A specific testable statement that predicts the expected outcome of the study
Alternative hypothesis for an experimental design (otherwise known as an experimental hypothesis)
An experimental hypothesis predicts a d_____ between two condition groups.
Alternative hypothesis for a non-experimental design
Non-experimental research, e.g., interviews and observations, may not be analysed quantitatively and so will not predict a difference or association. Instead, the hypothesis will predict what the researcher expects to o_____r or the th_____ (patterns of response) the researcher expects to discover.
Alternative hypothesis for a correlational design
A correlational hypothesis predicts an a_____n or r_____p between two variables. It is a special kind of non-experimental hypothesis. There is a _____ correlation between _____ and _____ = formula for correlational hypothesis. The sign is optional depending on whether the hypothesis is directional or not.
Directional and non-directional hypotheses
Hypotheses are either directional or non-directional. A directional hypothesis predicts the direction of the difference (experimental) or relationship (correlation), whereas a non-directional hypothesis predicts that there is a difference or relationship but not the direction of the difference or relationship.

Now see if you can write the examples as both non-directional (1–3) and directional (4–6) hypotheses.

Ψ 1.

Ψ 2.

Ψ 3.

Ψ 4.

Ψ 5.

Ψ 6.

Null hypothesis

Null hypothesis for an experimental design

Predicts n_ d_____ between the two condition groups. The IV has no effect on the DV, e.g., there will be no significant difference between X and Y and any differences that do exist are due to chance and/or random variables.

Null hypothesis for a correlational design

Predicts n_ r_____ between the two variables, e.g., there is no correlation between X and Y and any association that does exist is due to chance and/or random variables.

Null hypothesis for a non-experimental design

Predicts that the observed behaviour or pattern of response will not occur. Thus, transfers the statement into the negative.

Analysis of the results will reveal whether a significant difference or relationship does exist. If results prove significant the experimental or correlational hypothesis is a_____ and the null hypothesis is r_____.

Finally, write a null hypothesis for each of the examples.

Ψ 1.

Ψ 2.

Ψ 3.

Ψ 4.

Ψ 5.

Ψ 6.

Using this in the exam

Exam questions may ask you to state the aim or hypothesis based on the stimulus in the question. The hypothesis will usually be experimental or correlational (so ask yourself: is a difference or a relationship being investigated, and make sure you use the correct term). For example:

Suggest a suitable <u>aim/directional/non-directional/null hypothesis</u> for this investigation. (2 marks)

Note that the question above indicates the direction of the hypothesis. However, you could be asked to identify whether the hypothesis is directional or non-directional. For example:

State whether your hypothesis is directional or non-directional and justify your choice. (3 marks)

EXAM TIP: Where underlining occurs, only one of the terms would be given in the question.

Variables

For details, see Eysenck's textbook (page 298) and Brody and Dwyer's revision guide (page 136).

Experimental variables
Experiments involve two variables: the IV (independent variable) and the DV (dependent variable). The experimenter *manipulates* the IV (or it varies naturally) and *measures* the DV. The IV has a specified effect on the DV and so changes in the IV will result in changes in the DV.

Correlational variables
Correlational investigations involve two co-variables V1 and V2. These co-variables are associated but because of the lack of control it cannot be ascertained if they are causally related.

The variables are specified in the hypothesis.

Following the example below, test your knowledge of hypotheses and variables by stating whether the following hypotheses are: 1) experimental or correlational, 2) directional or non-directional, and 3) identify either the IV and DV, or V1 and V2.

Delete the incorrect hypotheses and variables, and fill in the blanks. The first one is a completed example.

1. There is a gender difference in the percentage of conformity on Asch's line experiment.
   Alternative hypothesis: Experimental/~~Correlational~~   ~~Directional~~/Non-directional
   Variables: IV/~~V1~~= gender   DV/~~V2~~= percentage of conformity

2. There is a positive correlation between self-report measures of stress and anxiety.
   Alternative hypothesis: Experimental/Correlational   Directional/Non-directional
   Variables: IV/V1=_____   DV/V2=_____

3. Attachment type as measured by the Strange Situation varies between individualistic and collectivistic cultures.
   Alternative hypothesis: Experimental/Correlational   Directional/Non-directional
   Variables: IV/V1=_____   DV/V2=_____

4. Participants who use semantic processing will remember significantly more words from a previously memorised word list than those who use non-semantic processing.
   Alternative hypothesis: Experimental/Correlational   Directional/Non-directional
   Variables: IV/V1=_____   DV/V2=_____

5. There is a relationship between number of hours' sleep and self-report measures of mental alertness.
   Alternative hypothesis: Experimental/Correlational   Directional/Non-directional
   Variables: IV/V1=_____   DV/V2=_____

6. People with high authoritarian personality scores are significantly more obedient than people with low authoritarian personality scores.
   Alternative hypothesis: Experimental/Correlational   Directional/Non-directional
   Variables: IV/V1=_____   DV/V2=_____

7. There is an association between number of life events experienced and number of days' illness in previous 12 months.
   Alternative hypothesis: Experimental/Correlational   Directional/Non-directional
   Variables: IV/V1=_____   DV/V2=_____

8. Ratings of physical attractiveness of both members of a dating couple are associated.
   Alternative hypothesis: Experimental/Correlational   Directional/Non-directional
   Variables: IV/V1=_____   DV/V2=_____

Using this in the exam

Exam questions may ask you to identify the variables from the study described in the question stimulus. So know the difference between the IV and DV. For example:

What was the <u>independent variable/dependent variable</u> in this investigation?   (1 mark)

EXAM TIP: Where underlining occurs, only one of the terms would be given in the question.

Experimental Research Designs

For details, see Eysenck's textbook (page 300) and Brody and Dwyer's revision guide (page 146). Fill in the gaps using the letter clues provided and use the cues in the table to guide your note taking.

The three designs aim to control participant variation, i.e., i_____ d_____ between the participants, which could interfere with the effect of the IV on the DV. All three designs share a common characteristic of experiments: two c_____, and the IV is varied across these. This usually involves a c_____l condition, which is not exposed to the IV and so acts as a baseline, and an e_____l condition, which is influenced by the IV and so shows the effect of this in comparison to the control condition.

Independent design

Two groups of different participants. Thus, different participants in each of the conditions. Participants experience one condition.	**Strengths** Ψ Avoids order effects. Ψ Random allocation.	**Weaknesses** Ψ Participant variables. Ψ Number of participants.

Matched participants design

Participants in each condition are matched on a one-to-one basis on certain relevant variables. Participants experience one condition. Thus, there are two groups, but they are matched, and each experiences a different condition.	**Strengths** Ψ Avoids order effects. Ψ Minimises participant variables.	**Weaknesses** Ψ Does not eliminate participant variables. Ψ Difficult to achieve a good match.

Repeated measures design

Same participants in both conditions. There is one group of participants who take part in two conditions.	**Strengths** Ψ Minimises participant variables. Ψ Fewer participants are needed.	**Weaknesses** Ψ Order effects. Ψ Demand characteristics are easier to guess.

Using this in the exam

You need to be able to select an appropriate design. For example, if you wanted to test the effect of the make of football boots on performance, which design should be used?

Non-experimental Research Designs

Naturalistic observation

The following design factors need to be considered:

Ψ Overt or covert observation.

Ψ Participant or non-participant observation.

Ψ Event, time, and point sampling.

Ψ Recording the data, e.g., frequencies, observation criteria, notes, video or audio recordings.

Ψ Ethical considerations.

Interviews

The following design factors need to be considered:

Ψ Structured, semi-structured, or unstructured.

Ψ Constructing good questions.

Ψ Ethical considerations.

Questionnaires

The following design factors need to be considered:

Ψ Closed and open questions.

Ψ Ambiguity and bias.

Ψ Attitude scale construction.

Ψ Ethical considerations.

Using this in the exam

Identify the research design and give one advantage and one disadvantage of this.   (1 + 2 + 2 marks)
Suggest one disadvantage of this design and explain how this might be overcome.   (2 + 2 marks)
Describe the aims and procedures of a possible follow-up study (or of this study)...   (6 marks)
Any of the above designs could come up in the exam and you would also need to draw from the 'Factors associated with research design' worksheet.

Factors Associated with Research Design

For details, see Eysenck's textbook (page 302) and Brody and Dwyer's revision guide (page 148). Fill in the gaps using the letter clues provided and use the cues in the table to guide your note taking.

The following all need to be considered in the design of research to ensure that there are no serious flaws that will undermine the reliability and validity of the research. A lack of control can lead to: systematic or c_____ error, when one condition's experience is in some way different to the other's (e.g., one group tested in the morning and the other in the afternoon). OR un_____ or random error, when there is a lack of s_____ and participants' e_____ differ within and between conditions.

Operationalisation
In quantitative research the variables in the hypothesis must be defined precisely. That is, it must be clear how the variables will be measured. If the exam question asks you to operationalise the variables, explain how they can be measured.

Ψ Advantages of operationalisation.

Ψ Limitations of operationalisation.

Pilot study
This is a small-scale trial run of the main study.

Ψ Test materials.

Ψ Test procedure.

Control of experimental designs—the weaknesses of the designs are potential confounding variables

Independent design
Participant variables are the weakness of this design and these are controlled by large samples and random allocation.

Repeated measures design
Order effects are the weakness of this design and these are controlled by counterbalancing, e.g., ABBA. OR randomisation is an alternative to counterbalancing.

Further confounding variables and bias

Confounding variables interfere with the effect of the IV on the DV. The researcher cannot be confident that the change in the DV is due to the IV if confounding variables (called extraneous variables when controlled) are a source of constant error.

Ψ Situational variables.

Ψ Distraction and confusion.

The relationship between the researcher and participant

Ψ Demand characteristics and participant reactivity, e.g., evaluation apprehension, social desirability bias, the Hawthorne effect.

Ψ Investigator effects, e.g., experimenter expectancy.

Control of confounding variables and bias

Standardisation is used to ensure that all of the participants experience the same research process. Variables must be controlled and deception may be needed to avoid participant reactivity and investigator effects.

Ψ Hold confounding variables such as noise, temperature, and time of day constant.

Ψ Standardised instructions and procedures control for distraction and confusion, and participant reactivity and investigator effects. They also ensure research is replicable.

Control of participant reactivity and researcher effects

Ψ Single-blind procedure.

Ψ Double-blind procedure.

Using this in the exam

Identify two ways you could operationalise the IV in this study. (2 marks)
Explain what a pilot study is, why a pilot study should be conducted, and how you would carry this out. (2 + 2 + 2 marks)
Identify two potential confounding variables in the context of this study. (2 marks)
Explain two features of the study that might affect the validity of the data being collected. (2 + 2 marks)
Explain one way in which the relationship between the researcher and participant might have influenced the results obtained in this study. (2 marks)
Describe one way that investigator effects (or participant reactivity) might threaten the validity of your study and suggest a way to overcome this. (3 marks)
Describe one way that demand characteristics might influence your findings. (2 marks)

Reliability and Validity

For details, see Eysenck's textbook (page 304) and Brody and Dwyer's revision guide (pages 149–150). Fill in the gaps using the letter clues provided and use the cues in the table to guide your note taking.

Reliability and validity are used to judge the quality of research.

Reliability	
Reliability is based on c_____. If the research produces the same results every time it is carried out then it is reliable. **Internal reliability = consistency within the method** Ψ Measuring instruments. Ψ Reliability of observations.	Internal and external reliability can be checked using c_____ t_____. **Techniques to check internal reliability** Ψ Split-half technique. Ψ Inter-rater reliability (or inter-judge reliability).
External reliability = consistency between uses of the method Ψ Reliability of psychological tests.	**Techniques to check external reliability** Ψ Test–retest reliability.

Validity

Campbell and Stanley (1966) have distinguished between i_____ and e_____ validity.

Internal validity = does it measure what it set out to? Is the effect genuine?	**External validity = g_____ to other settings (e_____) and populations**
Ψ Experimental validity—is the IV really responsible for the effect on the DV?	Ψ Coolican (1994) identifies four main aspects to external validity: • Populations.
Ψ Coolican (1994) identifies many threats to internal validity, i.e., other factors that could have caused the effect on the DV: • Confounding variables. • Unreliable measures. • Standardisation. • Randomisation. • Demand characteristics. • Participant reactivity. Ψ Good research design increases internal validity.	• Locations. • Measures or constructs. • Times.
Checking internal validity Ψ Replication.	**Checking external validity** Ψ Meta-analyses.

Using this in the exam

You may be asked to identify ways to check reliability or validity, so learn the tests.

Identify one way in which you could ensure reliability/validity and explain how you would put this into practice.

(3 marks)

Sampling

For details, see Eysenck's textbook (page 307) and Brody and Dwyer's revision guide (page 152). Fill in the gaps using the letter clues provided and use the cues in the table to guide your note taking.

Research is conducted on people, and the group of people that the researcher is interested in is called the target p_____. However, it is usually not possible to use all of the people from here and so a s_____ must be selected. Those selected are called p_____ for research purposes.

Thus, research is conducted on a sample but the researcher hopes that the findings will be true (valid) for the target population. For this to happen the sample must be r_____ of the target population. If the sample is representative then the findings can be g_____ back to the target population. If not, the findings lack population v_____. Therefore, the key issue is the generalisability of the sample, and this is based on two key factors:

Ψ *Type* of sampling.   Ψ *Size* of the sample.

Random sampling
Ψ Random methods—every participant has an equal chance of being selected.
Evaluation

Opportunity sampling
Ψ Availability.
Evaluation

Volunteer sampling
Ψ Self-selected.
Evaluation

Sample size
There is no ideal number of participants, but a number of factors must be considered:
Ψ
Ψ
Ψ
Ψ
Golden rule

Using this in the exam

You could be asked to identify a method of sampling and to explain how you would implement it. Random sampling is the easiest way to ensure you access all of the marks, as you need to explain that this means 'every participant has an equal chance of being chosen' and then explain how to do this, e.g., random number table, or names out of a hat.

Suggest a suitable method for selecting participants and explain how you would carry this out.   (1 + 2 marks)

Qualitative Analysis of Data

For details, see Eysenck's textbook (page 314) and Brody and Dwyer's revision guide (page 135). Use the cues in the table to guide your note taking.

Qualitative data can be collected via naturalistic observation, interviews, and questionnaires.

Data can take many forms:

Ψ

Ψ

Ψ

Thus, the data is words, not numbers, and the emphasis is on meaning.

Principles of qualitative analysis
Ψ Gather data.
Ψ Consider categories suggested by participants.
Ψ Analyse the meanings, attitudes, and interpretations, e.g., DISCOURSE ANALYSIS.
Ψ Consider the research hypothesis and possibly how it has changed as a result of the investigation.
Ψ Making qualitative data quantitative, e.g., CONTENT ANALYSIS.
Evaluation

Quantitative Analysis of Data

See Eysenck's textbook (page 316) and Brody and Dwyer's revision guide (pages 135 and 154). Follow the instructions in the table and practise the calculations.

Descriptive statistical techniques summarise the data. Measures of central tendency and dispersion are descriptive statistics. The findings can also be summarised using graphs. However, to decide which is the appropriate measure or graph to use, the level of measurement must first be established.

Level of measurement listed in order of increasing precision (note the acronym: NOIR)
<u>N</u>ominal:
<u>O</u>rdinal:
<u>I</u>nterval:
<u>R</u>atio:
Measures of central tendency
You may have heard of the three measures before; they are averages, and so involve the calculation of a single number representative of the other numbers it is associated with. The average is the central point in the score distribution.
MODE—the number that occurs most frequently. **Advantage:** Quick and easy to calculate and can be used whatever the level of data. **Limitations:** This is not widely used in psychological research as it is subject to great variability and provides very limited information. It does not tell us about the other values in the score distribution. A further problem is that it is possible to have more than one modal value; two modal values are known as **bimodal values**, and more than two are called **multi-modal**. Calculate the mode in the example below. E.g., 2 4 5 5 6 6 6 7 8 10
MEDIAN—the **middle value** when the scores are arranged from lowest to highest. Half the values in a score distribution are above the median, and half below it. When there is an even number of scores the two middle values are added together and then divided by two. **Advantages:** Can be used when you are unsure about the **reliability** of the extreme values and when you have **skewed distributions**. It can be used with **ordinal** or **interval** levels of measurement. **Limitations:** The median is susceptible to minor alterations (variability) in the data set (score distribution). Calculate the median in the example below. E.g., 2 4 5 5 6 6 6 7 8 10
MEAN—this is the arithmetic average. To calculate, add all the values together and divide the total by the number of values. **Advantages:** This is the best measure to use as it makes use of all the data in the score distribution. **Limitations:** It is fine when the data forms a normal distribution (remember the bell-shaped curve) but when there are extreme outlying values (anomalies) the mean value is easily distorted and so the median should be used instead. The mean should only be used for data of interval or ratio measurement. Calculate the mean in the example below. E.g., 2 4 5 5 6 6 6 7 8 10

Measures of dispersion

These measure the variability within the data distribution, i.e., are the scores similar to each other or different? Thus, they are a measure of the spread of the scores in the data distribution.

Variation ratio—This complements the mode; it is the proportion of non-modal scores.

E.g., 2 3 6 6 6 7 7 8 8 10
Mode = 6

Proportion of non-modal scores $= \dfrac{7}{10} \times 100$
So variation ratio = 70

Advantages: It is easy to calculate.

Limitations: This has the same key disadvantage as the mode; it is not representative of all scores in the distribution and so tends not to be used.

Calculate the variation ratio in the example below.
E.g., 1 3 3 4 6 6 7 7 7 7 8 9 9 9 10

Range—This is the difference between the highest and lowest scores in a data set.

1 is added if the scores are all whole numbers.

0.5 is added if values are recorded to the nearest half.

0.1 is added if the values are recorded to one decimal place.

Advantages: It is easy to calculate.

Limitations: The two most extreme values are used to calculate the range, so if these are outlying, the calculated range will not be representative of the distribution. It does not make use of all the data in the score distribution.

Calculate the range in the example below.
E.g., 1 3 3 4 6 6 7 7 7 7 8 9 9 9 10

Interquartile range—This solves the problem of outlying values as only the middle 50% of scores are used in the calculation. It also gives a better idea of the distribution of values around the centre.

Calculate the interquartile range in the example below.
E.g., 1 3 3 4 6 6 7 7 7 7 8 9 9 9 10

Standard deviation—This is a measure of variability, which measures scores in terms of difference from the mean.

Advantages: As with the mean, the standard deviation uses all the scores in a set of data and so is the best measure of dispersion to use. We can make inferences based on the relationship between the standard deviation and a normal distribution curve.

Limitations: It needs interval or ratio levels of measurement, and data to be approximately normally distributed.

Calculate the standard deviation in the example below.
E.g., 1 3 3 4 6 6 7 7 7 7 8 9 9 9 10

1. Calculate the mean.
2. Obtain the value of d (difference) by taking away the mean from each score.
3. Square all of the values of d and get the sum total of all of the values of d squared.
4. Divide this result by one less than the number of participants to get the variance.
5. Calculate s (standard deviation) by taking the square root of the variance.

Graphs and Charts

For details, see Eysenck's textbook (page 322) and Brody and Dwyer's revision guide (page 156). Use the cues in the table to guide your note taking.

Graphs and charts present the data visually. They are a useful way of summarising information as the data is easily accessible in a visual format.

Types of graphs and charts
Histograms Ψ Sketch an example of a histogram.   The histogram is used to present frequencies in the data. The data should be measured at interval or ratio level for the histogram to be appropriate. Scores are presented on the x-axis and the frequencies on the y-axis. Frequencies are represented by rectangular columns in the histogram.
Bar charts Ψ Sketch an example of a bar chart.   Also widely used, bar charts illustrate data measured at nominal or ordinal level. They are used for non-continuous variables and so the bars are separate from each other. Compare them with the histogram where the bars are adjoined. They are often used to illustrate the means from different conditions.

Scattergraphs

Ψ Sketch an example of a scattergraph.

Positive correlation   **No correlation**   **Negative correlation**

Scattergraphs are used to present correlated data. It does not matter which variable goes on which axis. Correlations range from perfect positive (+1), to no correlation, to perfect negative (–1). The sign indicates the direction, and the correlation coefficient (the number) indicates the strength of the correlation. If scores are positively correlated they increase together. If they are negatively correlated, as the scores on one variable increase the scores on the other variable decrease. Perfect positive and perfect negative correlations are rare in psychological research. Imperfect correlations are more common, for example, +0.7 is an imperfect positive correlation and –0.4 is an imperfect negative correlation. The closer the correlation coefficient is to 1, the stronger the correlation.

Using this in the exam

You may be asked to interpret any of the above graphs in the exam. So make sure you are clear on how to interpret them. You may be tested on which graph you would select to represent data, so read the uses of each graph again so you know when each graph is most appropriate. You could also be asked to select an appropriate qualitative or quantitative method of analysis and to explain how you would carry this out.

Identify a suitable graph or chart that could be used to illustrate the data in Table 1 and give one reason why this would be an appropriate descriptive method. (1 + 1 marks)

State one or two conclusions that can be drawn from the data in Figure 1/Table 1 and use this data to explain your answer. (2 marks or 4 marks)

Describe an appropriate method for analysing the data, why this is an appropriate method, and how you would put this into practice. (2 + 2 + 2 marks)

Research Methods Revision

Use this as a checklist and tick off as you feel confident you can answer the different types of question.

Types of exam question

Ψ The Method question

☐

For example: Identify the research method used in this investigation and explain one advantage and one disadvantage of this method. (1 + 2 + 2 marks)

You need to be able to identify the method being used from the question and give advantages and disadvantages of this method. So can you give two advantages and two disadvantages for each method?

Please remember that not all research is experimental. It may be wisest if you refer to all research as 'the study' so as not to make the mistake of calling a non-experimental method 'the experiment'.

Ψ The Research Design question

☐

For example: Identify the research design used in this investigation and explain one advantage and one disadvantage of this design. (1 + 2 + 2 marks)

Describe the aims and procedures of a possible follow-up study (or of this study). (6 marks)

Any of the research designs could come up and you would also need to draw from the 'Factors associated with research design' worksheet.

Know the difference between independent measures (two different groups of participants), repeated measures (one group of participants who experience both conditions), and matched participants (same as independent but the participants are matched). Know the advantages and disadvantages, e.g., participant variables and order effects, and know the controls for these (see random allocation and counterbalancing questions). Also, know how to implement and evaluate the non-experimental research designs. The aims/procedures question is particularly important as there are 6 marks for this question, so draw from 'Research methods' and the APFCCs you have came across in the other topics to recognise what should be included in this question (see the APFCC template).

Ψ The Aims/Hypothesis question

☐

For example: Describe an aim/directional hypothesis/non-directional/null hypothesis of this investigation. (2 marks per question)

Can you give an experimental (significant difference) hypothesis, a correlational (significant correlation/ relationship) hypothesis, and a null hypothesis? Decide whether the hypothesis is directional or non-directional and justify your choice, i.e., refer to previous research.

Ψ The Operationalisation question

☐

For example: Identify two ways in which you could operationalise... (2 marks)

How can the variables be measured, e.g., frequencies (nominal), rating scale (ordinal)? You need to be able to explain the operations, e.g., operationalise risk-taking behaviour.

Ψ The Variable question

☐

For example: Identify the IV or DV, or both, in this investigation. (1 mark or 2 marks)

Experimental: The IV is the variable manipulated or controlled by the experimenter, or naturally occurring (e.g., age, gender, culture). The DV is the variable that is measured to show the effect of the IV. Don't describe what an IV or DV is as I have done here. Instead use this information to help you identify the variables from the question stimulus.

Correlational: V1 and V2. It does not matter which variable is 1 or 2 so just identify the two co-variables that are associated.

Ψ The Investigator Effects question

For example: Describe one way that investigator effects might threaten the validity of your study.

(2 marks)

Researcher-bias when setting the research question (formulation), in the carrying out of the research (e.g., giving away the demand characteristics and the researcher expectancy effect), in the analysis of the results (manipulation of the data), and in the interpretation of the data.

Ψ The Participant Reactivity question

For example: Describe one way that participant reactivity might threaten the validity of your study.

(2 marks)

This occurs when participants respond to the demand characteristics, which are cues in the research situation, or given away by the researcher, that might reveal the research hypothesis.

Participant reactivity includes the co-operative participant who tries to guess the research hypothesis in order to comply with it, or the negativistic participant who tries to guess the research hypothesis in order to work against it. Participants may also show evaluation apprehension, which can lead to the social desirability effect, or the Hawthorne effect, that is, participants' behaviour changes as a consequence of being researched.

Ψ How to Control Investigator Effects/Participant Reactivity question

For example: Explain one way to overcome investigator effects/participant reactivity.

(2 marks per question)

Single-blind procedure controls for participant reactivity, as this is where the hypothesis is withheld from the participant and so they are not aware which condition they are in. This reduces demand characteristics.

Double-blind procedure controls for researcher expectancy as this involves a research assistant who collects the data without any knowledge of the research hypothesis. Thus, neither the researcher nor the participants know the research hypothesis and so the expectancy effect is controlled.

Ψ The Confounding Variables question

For example: Explain two features of the study that might have affected the validity of the data being collected.

(2 + 2 marks)

If the question asks you to identify confounding variables, ask yourself what other variables could have affected the DV other than the IV? Will it have a systematic or unsystematic effect?

Participant variables: Give an example of an individual difference that is relevant to the study described in the question.

Situational variables: Give an example of an environmental difference that is relevant to the study described in the question.

Ψ The Standardisation question

For example: Explain one way to control for confounding variables.

(2 marks)

Standardised procedures and instructions are used to ensure the research conditions are the same for all participants. This avoids some participants being treated more favourably than others, or some participants being given more demand characteristics than others, or some participants experiencing more distraction and confusion than others.

Ψ The Pilot Study question

For example: Explain what a pilot study is, why a pilot study should be conducted, and how you would carry this out. (2 + 2 + 2 marks)

A pilot study is carried out to trial run the materials and procedure to identify any flaws or areas for improvement that can then be corrected before the main study, e.g., clarity of instructions, ambiguity of questions, timing, clarity of the procedure.

Ψ The Sample question

For example: Suggest a suitable method for selecting participants and explain how you would carry this out and why it is an appropriate method for this investigation. (1 + 2 + 2 marks)

Which sample would you use? Why? And how?

Random sampling would be used because every participant in the target population has an equal chance of being chosen. Therefore it is less biased and is considered more representative of the target population. Use random number tables, a computer that generates random numbers, or names out of a hat to achieve a random sample.

Opportunity sampling is when you sample whoever is available. The fact that it is left to the researcher's discretion to approach whoever is available leaves room for bias as the researcher may sample people on the basis that they find them attractive or think they look approachable.

Ψ The Random Allocation question

For example: Explain how you would control for the weaknesses of the independent measures design. (2 marks)

This refers to how the participants are allocated to conditions in the independent measured design. As with the random sample it is best if every participant has an equal chance of being allocated to the condition. This reduces bias and minimises participant variables, but does NOT eliminate them.

Ψ The Counterbalancing question

For example: Explain how you would control for the weaknesses of the repeated measures design. (2 marks)

This refers to how the participants are allocated to conditions in the repeated measures design. It controls for order effects such as guessing the demand characteristics, practice, or fatigue, which may occur if all participants experience the two conditions in the same order. The ABBA design controls for this because half experience A then B and the other half experience B then A. This balances out the order effects across the two conditions but does NOT eliminate them.

Ψ The Validity question

For example: Identify one way in which you could ensure validity and explain how you would put this into practice. (3 marks)

The external validity might be affected, i.e., the results may not generalise to other settings (ecological validity), people (population validity), or periods in time (temporal validity). Internal validity, i.e., did you measure what you claimed to? Researcher effects, participant reactivity, confounding variables, and experimental realism all decrease validity because the observed effect may be due to one of these and not the IV. Check for validity: replicate with different populations or in different contexts, e.g., replication and meta-analysis.

Ψ The Reliability question

For example: Identify one way in which you could ensure reliability and explain how you would put this into practice. (3 marks)

Consistency within the research is internal reliability, and between uses of the measure is external reliability, e.g., over time.

Check for reliability: replicate to see if the results are consistent over time, test–retest, or check that there is consistency between two observers, inter-observer reliability/inter-rater reliability.

Ψ The Data Analysis question

For example: Describe an appropriate method for analysing the data, why this is an appropriate method, and how you would put this into practice. (2 + 2 + 2 marks)

Identify a suitable graph or chart that could be used to illustrate the data in Table 1 and give one reason why this would be an appropriate descriptive method. (1 + 1 marks)

State one or two conclusions that can be drawn from the data in Figure 1/Table 1 and use this data to explain your answer. (2 or 4 marks)

Quantitative analysis—measures of central tendency and dispersion: know how to interpret the average and the spread of the score distribution. Also know levels of measurement (nominal, ordinal, interval, ratio). Practise interpreting graphs and tables and make sure you can select appropriate graphs and charts, e.g., a scattergraph for correlated data, or a bar chart for discontinuous data.

Qualitative analysis—the stimulus study may be investigating meanings and so a qualitative analysis is more appropriate. Make sure you know the principle of qualitative analysis and can describe how to carry out discourse analysis and content analysis.

Ψ The Quantitative vs. Qualitative Approach question

For example: Give an advantage and a disadvantage of the quantitative/qualitative approach. (2 + 2 marks per question)

Give advantages and disadvantages for each. For example, quantitative is scientific and so it is replicable and therefore has high reliability, but it is descriptive and tends to lack validity. Qualitative gathers in-depth data that is high in validity but is difficult to replicate and so lacks reliability.

Ψ The Ethics question

For example: Identify one (or two) ethical issues that might have arisen in this investigation, and explain how the researcher might have dealt with them. (2 + 2 marks or 4 + 4 marks)

Identify two ethical issues. State which guidelines have been broken and why it is an issue in relation to the study in the question. Similarly, if asked to give two ethical considerations state two guidelines and why they should be observed. Be careful you do not state that you need informed consent when the hypothesis has been deliberately withheld. Deception, informed consent, and protection of participants are the main guidelines to consider.

Research Methods Crib Sheets

Cross-reference with Brody and Dwyer's revision guide and Eysenck's textbook.

Research methods
Experiment:
Correlation:
Observation:
Questionnaire:
Interview:

Factors associated with design
Operationalisation:
Standardisation:
Randomisation:
Pilot study:
Participant reactivity:
Investigator effects:
Single- and double-blind procedures:
Sample: A representative group of the target population:
Random:
Opportunity:

Research design
Experiment:

Independent measures: ....
....

Repeated measures: ....
....

Matched participants: ....
....

Observation: ....
....

Questionnaire: ....
....

Interview: ....

Reliability = consistency

Internal reliability: ....
....

Test: Split-half technique: ....
....

Inter-rater reliability: ....
....

External reliability: ....
....

Test–retest method (replication): ....

Validity = true

Internal validity: ....
....

External validity: ....

Ecological validity: ....

Population validity: ....

Temporal validity: ....
....

Reliability and validity are interlinked, as if the research is reliable it is likely to be valid, and if valid replicable and thus reliable.

Aims/hypotheses

Experimental = differences: ....
....

Correlational = association or relationship: ....
....

Non-experimental: ....

Null hypothesis: ....
....

Directional and non-directional: ....
....

Variables: ....
....

Experimental: IV: .... DV: ....
....

Correlational: V1, V2: ....

Data analysis

Qualitative analysis: ....
....

Discourse analysis: ....
....

Content analysis: ....
....

Evaluation: ....
....

Quantitative analysis—descriptive statistics
Measures of central tendency: ....
....

Measures of dispersion: ....
....

Levels of measurement: ....
....

Graphs and charts: ....
....

Histograms: ....
....

Bar charts: ....
....

Scattergraphs: ....
....

Evaluation: ....
....

Quantitative vs. qualitative approach: ....
....

Appendix 1: How to Impress the Examiner on AO2

The methodological criticisms in the table below are a useful source of AO2 marks and can also be used in AO1 evaluation questions. The criticisms of the research methods are also relevant to the 'Research methods' section of this workbook.

Examples have been given to show how the criticisms can be related to different topic areas. Fill in some of your own examples in the spaces provided. Positive and negative criticisms have been suggested—note the expression on the face!

<table>
<tr><td colspan="2" align="center">**Know the jargon and use it!**</td></tr>
<tr><td colspan="2">**EXPERIMENTAL**</td></tr>
<tr><td>☺</td><td>Variables are controlled and so have high internal validity and can infer cause and effect. Can easily replicate to verify reliability, e.g., behaviourism/learning theory (the scientific perspective!).</td></tr>
<tr><td>☹</td><td>Artificiality—may elicit the demand characteristics that can threaten internal validity, e.g., Loftus' (1974) research.</td></tr>
<tr><td>☹</td><td>External validity—may not generalise well to other settings, e.g., from the laboratory environment to real-life settings. Research lacks mundane realism, e.g., Milgram's (1963, 1974) research.</td></tr>
<tr><td colspan="2">Other examples include:

Compare with field and quasi-experiments.</td></tr>
<tr><td colspan="2">**CORRELATIONAL**</td></tr>
<tr><td>☺</td><td>Enables us to see association of variables that cannot be manipulated as an IV, e.g., divorce, and the effect of this on development.</td></tr>
<tr><td>☹</td><td>Causation cannot be inferred, as an IV has not been manipulated, e.g., stress and illness.</td></tr>
<tr><td>☹</td><td>Other factors/variables may be involved in the relationship, e.g., individual differences in the relationship between stress and illness.</td></tr>
<tr><td colspan="2">Other examples include:</td></tr>
</table>

SELF-REPORT (Questionnaires and interviews)

☺ Economical and practical, a high response can easily be obtained.

☹ Interviewer bias—the formation of questions, implementation (carrying out the research), analysis, and interpretation can all threaten the validity (truth) of the research.

☹ Social desirability bias—people's answers may be distorted because they want to present themselves favourably.

☹ Only information that people are consciously aware of can be extracted; people are often unaware of why they behave in a certain way.

Other examples include:

OBSERVATION

☺ Can gain in-depth data of natural behaviour, which therefore has high validity.

☹ Ethics—if the observation is covert (the participants are not aware they are being watched).

☹ Participant reactivity (the Hawthorne effect)—participants' behaviour may change if they know they are being watched.

Other examples include:

CASE STUDY

☺ In-depth data that consequently has high internal validity as it tends to be meaningful and truthful.

☹ Based on clinical interviews that may be biased, and so internal validity may be questionable.

☹ Limited external validity (population validity) as the findings obtained from one individual are unlikely to be the same for another. Thus, there is low generalisability (external validity), e.g., privation cases such as Genie.

Other examples include:

SAMPLE SIZE

🙁 Sample bias—samples that are small, self-selected, or selected on the basis of availability (opportunity sampling), ethnocentric (centred around a specific ethnic type, e.g., a sample involving only Western, white, middle-class Americans is culturally biased), androcentric (male-centred), or only involve a restricted population, all lack generalisability because they are not very representative and so are biased samples. The results would have low population validity, as generalisability to other populations would be limited. For example, the social influence studies of Milgram (1963, 1974) and Asch (1952) were self-selected, ethnocentric, and androcentric.

Other examples include:

CONFOUNDING VARIABLES

🙁 Participant variables—e.g., individual differences in stress and attachments.

🙁 Situational variables—factors in the environment affecting the results, e.g., distraction, noise, temperature, time of day.

Other examples include:

Confounding variables threaten internal validity, as in an experiment the IV may not be responsible for the effect on the DV if confounding variables are not controlled. In a correlation, other factors besides the two variables being investigated may be involved in the association.

VALIDITY

Internal validity—the validity of the research within the research context. If research is valid it is likely to be reliable.

🙂 If research has internal validity then it is assumed that it has truth. The effect or relationship on the DV, which is caused by the IV, is psychologically real. Therefore, the research measured what it set out to rather than some other factor such as bias or confounding variables.

Other examples include:

External validity—the validity of the research outside the research context.

☹ Ecological validity—lacks generalisability to other settings, e.g., Loftus (1974).

☹ Population validity—lacks generalisability to other populations, e.g., if it uses WWMCA as 90+% of all research does (Western, white middle-class, American sample; remember as modified YMCA).

☹ Temporal validity—lacks generalisability to other time periods as the research may be dated. The date of the research is a possible evaluation point. Contextualise the historical, political, social, and cultural contexts.These can influence the research and so it may lack generalisability to the current context. For example, Bowlby's (1946) research reflected the historical, social, and cultural context, and also the political agenda of the time.

☹ Real-life applications of the research—does the theory or explanation work in real-life? Does it have truth and so does it have value? Does the work add to our understanding? You should assess this on all essay questions.

Other examples include:

RELIABILITY

☺ If research has reliability it has consistency, e.g., the same results are produced over time or by different researchers. Repeating the research is called replication. This is used to establish reliability and validity as replication is usually only possible if the research has internal validity.

☺ Lack of consistency means that validity must also be questioned, e.g., the contradictory psychodynamic explanation of eating disorders. Whereas reliability supports validity as it suggests that the results are psychologically real.

Other examples include:

VALUE FREE vs. VALUE LADEN

☹ Research should not be distorted by researcher bias, it should be free from value judgements (objective not subjective). However, gender, culture, and nature bias all demonstrate value judgements. It can be argued that all research is value laden to some extent.

Other examples include:

DETERMINISM

☹ Biological determinism—the biological approach claims behaviour is determined by the genes, and so ignores the free will of the individual to determine their own behaviour.

☹ Physiological determinism—an explanation that claims physiological processes determine behaviour, and so ignores free will, e.g., hormonal imbalances or brain dysfunction as explanations of abnormality.

☹ Environmental determinism—the behavioural approach claims behaviour is determined by the environment, and so ignores free will, e.g., behaviourism/learning theory.

☹ Psychic determinism—the psychodynamic approach claims adult behaviour is determined by early childhood experience and that behaviour is determined by biological instincts and so ignores free will.

Other examples include:

REDUCTIONISM

☹ Oversimplified explanations that explain a complex phenomenon in terms of only one component. Biological (evolutionary), physiological, and environmental are all forms of reductionism and the above examples for determinism apply. Research may also be criticised for experimental reductionism, e.g., Asch's (1952) study of majority influence and the memory experiments in the 'Human memory' section of this workbook.

Other examples include:

NATURE/NURTURE

☹ Research often takes one perspective at the expense of the other. For example, biological explanations of eating disorders can be criticised for ignoring nurture and vice versa for the psychological explanations.

☺ A compromise position between nature and nurture is offered by the diathesis–stress model, and this interactionist perspective of the influence of genes and the environment offers a more comprehensive approach to understanding behaviour.

Other examples include:

ETHICS

☺ A cost–benefit analysis should precede all research. This involves deciding 'do the ends justify the means?'

☹ The breaking of ethical guidelines (deception, informed consent, right to withdraw, confidentiality, protection of participants) and socially sensitive research (research that has consequences for vulnerable groups, e.g., gender or culturally biased research) may be considered ethically injustifiable. For example, ethics is the critical issue in the 'Social influence' section so Milgram's (1963, 1974) and Asch's (1952) research can be criticised on ethical grounds.

Other examples include:

Essay questions require much more than a list of evaluation points, so please contextualise the above criticisms. You must fully relate any of the criticisms you use to the question to make sure they are relevant and not just add-ons. The latter, of course, might constitute good evaluation but would receive few marks if it does not answer the question. So assess the consequences of the criticisms by asking yourself: so what does this mean in terms of the question? Thus, make conclusions with respect to the question throughout your answer. For example, if validity is questioned you can conclude that the theory/research/explanation may lack truth and so explanatory power is limited as it does not offer meaningful insights. Elaborating the criticism like this gains more credit than simply identifying strengths and weaknesses.

See the 'Step-by-step guide to answering exam questions' in the 'Basics' section for more information on essay technique.

Appendix 2: Findings/Conclusions

Complete these and you will be prepared for questions that ask for findings (6 marks), or conclusions (6 marks). Cross-reference with the APFCCs as the studies here are to supplement the findings and conclusions in the APFCCs so that you have enough content for 6 marks on either aspect. Remember to convert what is in the textbook into your own words. Also make sure that you don't confuse conclusions with findings as this is a common mistake in the exam.

Findings are facts

Outline results and give percentages, etc. These are indisputable.

Conclusions are opinions

Ask: What do the results mean? Conclusions are the inferences/implications you draw from the results and are disputable.

To make sure you are giving conclusions and not findings begin your description with, 'The results show that…' or 'The research suggests…'.

You could also include the applications (uses) of the research.

Human Memory

Research into the nature of STM, e.g., Glanzer and Cunitz (1966) See Eysenck's textbook (page 45)	
Findings	**Conclusions**

Research into the nature of LTM, e.g., Cohen and Squire (1980)
See Eysenck's textbook (page 53)

Findings

Conclusions

Research into eyewitness testimony, e.g., Loftus and Zanni (1975)
See Eysenck's textbook (page 32)

Findings

Conclusions

Research into reconstructive memory, e.g., Cohen (1981) See Eysenck's textbook (page 78)	
Findings	**Conclusions**

Research into eyewitness testimony, e.g., follow-up research by Loftus and Palmer (1974) See Eysenck's textbook (page 79)	
Findings	**Conclusions**

Attachments in Development

<table>
<tr>
<td colspan="2" align="center">Research into individual differences,
e.g., Ainsworth et al. (1978), Ainsworth (1982), and
Main and Solomon (1986)
See Eysenck's textbook (pages 96–97)</td>
</tr>
<tr>
<td>Findings</td>
<td>Conclusions</td>
</tr>
<tr>
<td>

</td>
<td> </td>
</tr>
<tr>
<td colspan="2" align="center">Research into cultural variation, e.g., Sagi et al. (1991)
and Grossmann et al. (1985)
See Eysenck's textbook (page 100)</td>
</tr>
<tr>
<td>Findings</td>
<td>Conclusions</td>
</tr>
<tr>
<td>

</td>
<td> </td>
</tr>
</table>

Research into long-term effects of deprivation/separation, e.g., Bowlby et al. (1956)

See Eysenck's textbook (page 120)

Findings	Conclusions

Research into the effects of privation, e.g., Genie—Curtiss (1989), Rutter (1981), and Freud and Dann (1951)

See Eysenck's textbook (pages 121–123)

Findings	Conclusions

Stress

Research into stress and coronary heart disease (CHD), e.g., Ganster et al. (1991) and Matthews et al. (1977)
See Eysenck's textbook (page 164)

Findings	Conclusions

Research into stress and the immune system, e.g., Cohen et al. (1991) and Kiecolt-Glaser (1984)
See Eysenck's textbook (pages 144, 147)

Findings	Conclusions

Research into life changes, e.g., Rahe and Arthur (1977) and Holmes and Rahe (1967)
See Eysenck's textbook (pages 152–153)

Findings	Conclusions

Research into workplace stressors, e.g., Shirom (1989) and Margolis and Kroes (1974)
See Eysenck's textbook (page 162)

Findings	Conclusions

Abnormality

Research into biological explanations of eating disorders e.g., Kendler et al. (1991) See Eysenck's textbook (page 212)	
Findings	**Conclusions**

Research into psychological explanations of eating disorders e.g., Jaeger et al. (2002) See Eysenck's textbook (page 222)	
Findings	**Conclusions**

Social Influence

Research into obedience, e.g., Milgram's (1974) variations
See Eysenck's textbook (page 244)

Findings	Conclusions

Research into majority influence/conformity, e.g., Zimbardo (1973)
See Eysenck's textbook (pages 231–233)

Findings	Conclusions

Research into minority influence, e.g., Nemeth et al. (1974)

See Eysenck's textbook (page 235)

Findings	Conclusions

NOTES